Rental Housing in California

Market Forces and Public Policies

The Third Annual Donald G. Hagman
Commemorative Conference

Cosponsored by
University of California, Los Angeles, Extension
The Public Policy Program *and*
The Lincoln Institute of Land Policy

Edited by
LeRoy Graymer
Joseph DiMento
Frank Schnidman

A Lincoln Institute of Land Policy Book

Published by
Oelgeschlager, Gunn & Hain
in association with the
Lincoln Institute of Land Policy

AUK5415- 3/,

International Standard Book Number: 0-89946-220-0

Library of Congress Catalog Card Number: 86-28540

Printed in the U.S.A.

Oelgeschlager, Gunn & Hain, Publishers, Inc.
131 Clarendon Street
Boston, MA 02116 U.S.A.

Publication of a manuscript by the Lincoln Institute of Land Policy signifies that it is thought to be worthy of public consideration but does not imply endorsement of conclusions or recommendations. Views expressed in Lincoln Institute publications should be understood to be solely those of the authors and should not be attributed to the Lincoln Institute, its directors, officers, or staff members, or to the organization that supported research leading to any such publication.

Library of Congress Cataloging-in-Publication Data

Donald Hagman Memorial Conference (3rd)

 Rental housing in California.
 Includes index.

 1. Rental housing — California. 2. Rent control — California. I. Graymer, LeRoy, 1932– . II. DiMento, Joseph F. III. Schnidman, Frank. IV. Lincoln Institute of Land Policy. V. Title.

HD7288.85.U62C22 1987 333.33′8 86–28540
ISBN 0-89946-220-0

Contents

Lincoln Institute Foreword

The Lincoln Institute of Land Policy is an educational institute dedicated to the development and exchange of ideas and information pertaining to land policy and property taxation. It is a school offering opportunities for instruction and research. It welcomes government officials, working practitioners, and students to the pursuit of advanced studies.

The Lincoln Institute is also a center for linking the university and the practice of government; for bringing together scholars, professionals, and officials; and for blending the theory and practice of land policy.

With these goals in mind, the Lincoln Institute has joined with the Public Policy Program of the University of California, Los Angeles Extension, and with others, to prepare and present an annual commemorative program honoring the late UCLA law and planning professor Donald G. Hagman. Don was a giant in the field of land policy and property taxation, and he had given freely of his time to assist the Lincoln Institute in organizing and running "cutting-edge" seminars for public officials, practitioners, and academics.

In honor of his memory, and to carry on some of the research he did not complete, LILP joins in sponsoring this annual program. Don had many close friends and professional acquaintances with whom he shared his thoughts on the future of land and tax policy. The sponsors of this annual event welcome program suggestions from you who shared with him where we should be going in these difficult and trying fields. Programs should be stimulating, entertaining, packed with substance . . . and hopefully come with a program title that can be reduced to a catchy acronym. After all, that's the way Don would have liked it.

Frank Schnidman
Senior Fellow
January 1987

1

Introduction: Rental Housing in California: The Themes of the Book

Joseph DiMento* and LeRoy Graymer**

A Focus on Rental Housing

This third volume in the Hagman commemorative series focuses on a concern central to Donald Hagman's legacy: the tensions between market forces and public policy in providing important resources for our citizenry. Rental housing availability, quality, and affordability is the focus of this volume. We approach the subject through several routes and call on the expertise of economists, planners, housing consultants, developers, and lawyers who have worked in the area of the development or regulation of rental housing.

In the five chapters that follow we ask whether recent market behavior indicates a boom in rental housing. We inquire into the forces, nationwide and local, that influence the development of rent structures. Authors speculate about the future of supply and demand for the rental unit and explore numerous strategies—from tax reforms to rent control—that have an impact on the availability and maintenance of rental housing. Finally, we describe the beneficiaries of these strategies and ask who subsidizes whom.

Why is rental housing a public issue? John Friedman, chair of the planning program at UCLA, gave one answer to that question at the commencement of the 1985 program. He said,

*University of California, Irvine, Calif.
**University of California, Los Angeles, Calif.

Housing is not like any other commodity . . . in the marketplace. . . . The American people long ago recognized the special quality of housing as a social need, and a social need is a claim by one group of people against the common resources and thus against all other needs. If the market were capable of satisfying this need for everyone, the problem would be solved. But the market is notoriously unable to solve the housing problem for an increasing number of people. . . . The issue, therefore, is affordable and decent housing for those whose needs are not being met by the uncontrolled operation of the market.

Friedman's assessment of the essentially public character of the rental housing issue is not shared by all who contribute to this volume. For example, Ira S. Lowry's analysis indicates that a competitive market in rental property does exist and tends to keep rents close to the general rate of inflation. In fact, among the older population as a whole incomes have risen more rapidly than rents. Lowry stated:

There is a preposterous notion abroad in the land that landlords have some kind of monopoly power in their dealings with tenants. Nothing could be further from the truth. In all but the smallest communities, rental housing is an intensely competitive industry. Within a metropolitan area such as Los Angeles, there are thousands of landlords each anxious to keep his units occupied. About a third of all renters move at least once during a year and some move more than once. Consequently, roughly 40 percent of all rented dwellings come on the market in the course of a year, offering thousands of alternatives to homeseekers.

These remarks by two contributors introduce the debate over the apparent roles of the private and public sectors in rental housing and the potential conflicts that exist between the two. Some of this discussion revolves around the question of how certain subgroups in our population are housed. This relates well to the discussion of rapidly changing demographic patterns that was the theme of the Second Donald G. Hagman Commemorative Conference, "The Urban Caldron."[1] The book resulting from that conference provides considerable insight into the changing composition of populations and the kinds of issues, including housing, that arise from these changing social patterns.

Our contributors reflect considerable disagreement on how and whether to provide and maintain affordable rental housing, a disagreement that is even reflected in statistics on the housing problem. Is there a crisis? Different facts are offered. For some the problem is real and significant. Other authors describe the problem as less compelling for certain groups in society. Nonetheless, no one doubts that for lower-income people, the rental housing issue is most central. We learn that California renters pay about 35 percent of their incomes for rent, a small increase from the 32 percent they paid in 1970. But we also learn that in certain places, such as the San Francisco Bay Area, rents have increased by 75 percent in four years. We learn that there has been a recent boomlet in the production of multifamily construction, but we find no consensus on how long that boomlet will continue and whether it is responsive to the needs of the poor. There are vastly different interpretations of one of the most debated public policies related to affordable rental housing: rent control. About 35 percent of California's rental units are under rent control programs, but contributors disagree on whether that is a good thing or reflects a policy that ultimately defeats the purpose of providing affordable housing to the most needy. We are introduced to different perspectives on whether the subsidy provided the recipients of rent control is substantial and on who is subsidizing whom. Whether there is a right to live affordably in a given community is another point of contention. Participants ask whether a citizen has a right to live in a coastal community. Is there a right to live in Beverly Hills, in Santa Monica, or just somewhere, decently, in the state of California?

Yet the contributors agree on several major points, as the following chapters develop. Foremost is the observation that a political consti-tuency does not exist for the creation of a comprehensive public policy regarding the construction and maintenance of affordable rental hous-ing. Local political coalitions may form for particular programs, such as rent control, but nationwide, a political base for meeting the congres-sional goal of providing decent housing for all Americans has not materialized. Secondly, our commentators agree that the building of multiple-unit housing does not directly translate to the meeting of the needs of the poor. Very different prospects exist for those of lower income depending on where they live in the state. All authors bemoan the absence of good data on availability and quality of rental units. Scanty data contributes to public policy based on theory and ideology rather than on fact. This volume attempts to draw on the limited data and studies available on these very sensitive issues.

The Federal Role in Rental Housing

Economist Anthony Downs of the Brookings Institution provides a back-drop for the subsequent chapters by offering a comprehensive analysis of federal policies that affect the supply of and the demand for rental housing. He cautions that the basic congressional goal of providing a decent home and a suitable living environment for every American family needs to be regarded essentially as an inspiration in light of government failure to provide necessary funding, but he nonetheless describes a significant federal role in influencing the creation of rental housing. He underscores the tensions existing between policies aimed at affecting supply and those that manipulate demand. A clear example is the need to improve the profitability of providing rental housing by increasing rents. Downs introduces a theme that will be picked up in later chapters—the nature of the political environment that results from the regional distribution of renters and landlords or owners. He reminds the reader that renters compose over 70 percent of the residents of New York City and over 80 percent of the residents of Santa Monica, a statistic particularly important in the analysis of policies that address rent control.

Downs describes the federal influences on both the flow of capital and the distribution of income affecting the rental market. He inventories and discusses historical trends in public sector interventions including those related to interest rates, credit markets, and taxes. In certain periods the federal government has sheltered mortgage lending by protecting thrift institutions from having to pay full market prices to obtain deposits from small-scale savers. Historically, this has allowed for below-market rates for mortgages during tight money periods. Downs estimates that about one-third of all renter households with incomes below 50 percent of their area median income were receiving federal housing subsidies as of 1981. He then addresses the implications of restoring the favored financial treatment of housing, and he offers observations on the desirability of federal intervention into housing markets. A potential federal role in combatting exclusionary land use controls and rent controls exists. While recognizing both the strengths and weaknesses of federal intervention, Downs concludes that some federal activities are desirable. For example, he would have the federal government offer housing vouchers (in the absence of the more desirable direct financial assistance), and he would convert the present approach of homeowner tax deduction benefits to tax credits. He would also reduce the rate used to compute the credit enough to pay for the voucher program. Downs recognizes that what he considers desirable will not always track on federal policy; this he predicts will be influenced by widespread pressure to adopt rent controls and to increase the supply of new federally subsidized housing.

Entering California: Rental Housing and its Future

Housing analyst and consultant Ira Lowry begins the analysis of the rental housing situation in California where 44 percent of the citizenry are renters. His is a comprehensive description covering housing quality, rental unit availability, and availability as a function of economic status.

Lowry's is also a provocative introduction to the challenge of rental housing supply. For example, he finds little support for the notion that renters are badly squeezed in California, and he attacks the contention that landlords have a monopoly power in the rental market. In fact, Lowry finds rental housing to be a highly competitive business and one in which rent/income ratios remained substantially the same during the decade 1970–1980. He addresses rental housing with little sense of crisis—in part because he recognizes that the boundary between rental and owner-occupied housing inventories is flexible. What is rental today may be owner-occupied tomorrow. He also argues that renting can be a better investment than owning a home if certain strategies are followed in the fiscal environment that has followed the 1970s speculative boom period for home ownership.

Lowry proceeds to address the future of this industry. He sees both the demand for rental housing and the per capita demand increasing as real income rises in California. Part of the Lowry analysis comes from his life-cycle understanding of renting. Renting is the tenure choice in early years after young people leave their parents' homes and in the elderly years. It is also the option available to new immigrants. So while home ownership is the preferred option of many Americans, demographic shifts, such as those described in *The Urban Caldron* make for increased pressures for more rental housing. These shifts are also reflected in a blurring of the distinction between owning and renting a unit, in part because the new populations are settling in smaller dwellings with less private outdoor space and with less responsibility for maintenance. Some of these characteristics are desired; others are necessitated.

Just as renting can be a sound investment strategy, being a landlord can be a risky affair. Lowry sees the risk as increasing because of factors ranging from restrictions on profitability imposed by state and local laws to increased civil and criminal liability of the landlord. Collectively, these factors will discourage investment in rental property and will lead to the expectation of a decline in the proportion of rental dwellings owned by casual investors or held as income property by the elderly. Resulting will be two kinds of successful rental property: "the cracker-box apartment building catering to recent immigrants" and the upscale condominium occupied by prosperous renters.

Whither the California Boomlet?

Fred Case of the Graduate School of Management at UCLA asks whether there is a boomlet in the California rental housing market. His answer must be qualified because available data are insufficient to answer the question precisely and because there are several different markets in California making any one answer inappropriate. Case does say that there is evidence for a modest housing boomlet, but linking a general boomlet to a rental housing phenomenon is not an easy task. He concludes that there is little relief in sight in the upward push of rent in California, in part because a significant amount of multifamily construction has been for cooperatives and condominiums—not for rental housing. (Case recognizes that a large percentage of condominiums are rented.)

Case then moves to a county analysis and finds that there will be continued high demand for high-density housing in the coastal counties, but this housing stock does not generally serve lower-income people. A ripple effect will continue to move employers and housing construction to the noncoastal areas. There will be rental boomlets in adjacent counties and in the inland counties—places that are presently underpopulated and yet maintain much of the attraction of living in California. Overall, Case is tentative in light of the historical difficulty in forecasting housing demand. Exogenous factors continue to get in the way, such as the monetary crunch of 1966 and inflation of the 1970s. Nonetheless, a reasonably strong housing market through the year 2000 is predictable.

Following the articles by Lowry and Case, commentators Ben Bartolotto of the Construction Industry Research Board, Bradley Inman of the Bay Area Council, and Fred Kahane of the Southern California Association of Governments engage in a dialogue with the authors and the audience. The comments cover the nature of the housing crisis, the quality of data available to analyze housing issues, and the causes and victims of the gap between the demand and supply of affordable rental housing.

Fair City? Strategies for Promoting Affordability

In Chapter 5, a panel of experts analyzes a case example of an attempt to provide affordable housing in a community of 200,000 people. That community is not atypical of California municipalities: it has experienced growth, has attracted high-technology industry, and has met the housing needs of its professionals. But its nonprofessional workers compete for only a small number of affordable units. In this case, panelists suggest and analyze various strategies that might move the community to meet the objective articulated in its general plan: "a decent home in a decent environment for all who work in the community." The six panelists comment on what can be done within a political context consisting of an active prorental housing citizens group, an antigrowth group, and a local government split on the question of whether to promote opportunities for development of affordable rental housing.

John Danner, an attorney in San Francisco who worked on the San Francisco Plan, suggests that a political and legal reconnaissance is a first step to determining how volunteer citizen groups should act to promote affordable housing. He suggests, in addition, that rezoning will be necessary and that concrete proposals for rental housing development are essential. He concludes that the issue of rental housing must be put into a larger political context to make it of greater interest to those with other municipal concerns.

Susan DeSantis, director of the California Department of Housing and Community Development, considers the problem of providing affordable rental housing to be one with both technical and political dimensions. She advocates the development of a broad-based coalition of interest groups to work on influencing decisionmakers through direct contacts and involvement in participative planning activities. Recognizing difficulties in attempts to achieve rezoning in some communities, she enumerates several changes in development regulations. These range from density bonuses to expedited agency processing of affordable multiple-unit projects. She also describes federal and state programs available to meet the objectives of promoting affordable housing, and she suggests means of defusing opposition at the local level to rental projects. The state's role in the latter activity must be indirect; but it is real, and DeSantis outlines several strategies California has used.

V. Fei Tsen is a housing development consultant in Oakland, California who has seen several successes in developing affordable rental housing. Her comments begin with the premise that housing for low-income people exists, but there is no such thing as low-cost housing. Tsen describes the three major tasks facing the developer of affordable housing. He or she must determine costs of building, costs of operating, and a means of closing the gap between the costs of providing housing and the revenues available from low- and moderate- income residents. She employs an example in Oakland to describe the components of development and operation costs. That project succeeded in housing people with median incomes of $16,000 (a family of four) for as low as $285 per month. Tsen then offers a bag of tools for closing the affordability gap; these include strategies for writing down the costs of land and for reducing the costs of capital. She ends with the message that no one technique will make a project affordable. A combination of strategies is essential; such a combination can only come when local government is committed to seek all available sources of support.

Henry Felder, a deputy assistant secretary for policy development and research at the United States Department of Housing and Urban Development, concludes that the federal programs for rental housing end where Fair City's problems begin. The reason is that the Reagan administration has emphasized providing housing for the worst case and has not developed programs for middle-income people. Felder describes voucher and rehabilitation programs and joint ventures between federal and local government; the latter aim to identify factors that have obstructed development of affordable housing. He also describes successes of federal programs with target groups that differ from those in the case study.

Fair City is "a case study of indifference," concludes Christine Minnehan, the federal relations coordinator for the California senate and a senior consultant in the senate. She undertakes a political analysis of the problem and finds little will to build affordable housing in the subject community. Her strategy would be one of making the political environment uncomfortable for those who support the status quo. One means would be to find a developer interested in pushing local government to expedite an affordable housing project, perhaps with the assistance of industry; business can easily be convinced that the present commuting patterns of Fair City workers are ultimately economically destructive.

Ralph Catalano, a professor at the University of California Irvine and a member of the city council in Irvine, also offers a political assessment: the city in this case can be influenced; the political situation is a positive factor. A legal intervention, for example to make zoning consistent with the general plan, may need to be held out as a threat, but Catalano has seen in his own city successes in providing affordable housing in a political environment more challenging than that of Fair City. He also points out that attitudes are changing; surveys reveal that, for reasons related to the desire to develop communities where one can live as well as work, the population is becoming more receptive to government intervention to provide rental housing.

Rent Control: Analysis and Debate

This volume ends with analysis of a strategy for providing affordable housing that is among the most controversial in this area of public policy: rent control. The chapter contains papers by two leading analysts and a lively dialogue among panelists and with the audience.

Michael Teitz leads off the chapter with a comparative analysis of rent control experiences in different localities. Teitz, who is Professor and Chair of the City and Regional Planning Department at the University of California, Berkeley, prefaces his findings with the conclusion that "rent control is more than simple regulation of the price of a commodity. It carries with it a range of meanings that give rise to passionately held views and often extreme rhetoric." Teitz tells us what we know about the development of rent control (quite a bit) and about its effects (very little). He gives an interesting history of the first rent control programs during national emergencies and then focuses on the second generation of controls that began in 1959. The chapter is a valuable source of information on the extent of controls and the variations in the rules and governance structures. California has thirteen cities that control standard residential units which account for 35 percent of all rental housing units. This analysis presents a compendium of the issues and analysis of the limited empirical evidence existing on the effects of controls on rent levels, on security of tenure, on landlord profits, on levels of maintenance, and on capital investment and new construction of rental units. It is not possible to generalize on the impacts because of the high degree of variability in the specific rules, how they are enforced, and the fact that little conclusive evidence exists on long-term impacts. Theories abound on these issues: data are scanty.

Teitz also provides some background on the Los Angeles rent stabilization study covered next in the Rabinowitz paper, and he makes several interesting comments on the politics of rent control. Most central to this volume is the recognition that the coalitions that develop around rent control policy are quite unstable.

In the second paper in this chapter Francine Rabinowitz presents a summary of a major study of the Los Angeles rent stabilization program. Rabinowitz is a consultant and a professor of public administration and urban and regional planning at the University of Southern California. She directed the 1984 Los Angeles rental housing study that investigated the impact of rent stabilization on tenants, landlords, and the rental housing stock in the city of Los Angeles. Rabinowitz takes an empirical look at the Los Angeles case, one which is not necessarily representative of other rent control programs. She reports that the City's program had little effect on the average rate of increase in rents when Los Angeles is compared with contiguous cities: The Los Angeles "rental housing market has traversed peaks and valleys to emerge at roughly the point that it would have reached without rent stabilization." The study estimated that once the program had routinized, the average rent bill savings was approximately seven dollars per month. In general no great subsidies were found, but sizable subsidies to some types of tenants were identified, depending on demographic characteristics and on whether the tenant moved during the period of stabilization.

Rabinowitz also describes only a modest economic impact on landlords, although she points out that this was not achieved smoothly; immediately following enactment of the rent control program, rates of return temporarily dipped noticeably. Similarly new construction fell dramatically at first but rebounded sharply over the years of the program. The Rabinowitz paper concludes with an analysis of the probable effects of six alternatives to regulating the maximum rent increases permitted by the Los Angeles ordinance.

Can public policy accommodate the diverse needs rent control programs affect? The dialogue following the Teitz and Rabinowitz papers revolves around this question. Commentators are Stephen Carlson, executive director of the California Housing Commission; Karl Manheim, a law professor at Loyola Law School and formerly a city attorney in Santa Monica; Joel Silverman, a property owner in Los Angeles and member of the board of directors of the Apartment Association of Greater Los Angeles; and Barbara Zeidman, who directed the city of Los Angeles rent stabilization program. The panelists question whether affordable housing is a right and how this right might be reconciled with previous ownership rights. The discussion then focuses on the interests affected by rent stabilization or control efforts. The concern is with the problem of untargeted beneficiaries of rent control who may reap windfalls from a policy that aims to assist those in financial need. Whether there are additional subsidies to those identified in the papers is discussed as is the question who should be subsidizing whom. The panelists also address some practical issues including the relationship between vacancy control and just cause eviction provisions in landlord-tenant law and the proper level of government for intervention into this area of housing policy. This discussion and this volume end with a thought-provoking quotation from a recent California Court of Appeal case: "it is just a matter of time before the remaining vacant space will be exhausted in every major city in California." What will public policy have to say about who occupies that scarce resource?

Notes

1. George Sternlieb, Center for Urban Policy Research of Rutgers University pointed out in his response to the first paper at the 1985 program that part of the housing problem is clearly demographic: "this country had an explosion of labor force in the last dozen years ending roughly around 1980 equivalent to the entire labor force of West Germany. In twelve years we absorbed about 28 million (people) in labor force."

2

The Federal Government: Future Rental Housing Policies

Anthony Downs *

The U.S. Congress has established as a basic goal for all federal housing policies "the realization as soon as feasible of . . . a decent home and a suitable living environment for every American family."[1] This goal was first stated in 1949 and has been reaffirmed for over thirty years, but has never been fully attained because Congress has not appropriated enough funds. Given the Reagan administration's drive to reduce federal non-defense spending, the realization of this goal is not likely to be feasible soon. Hence this goal must be regarded primarily as an aspiration, not as a guarantee that individual families can use to demand publicly financed fulfillment of their "rights" to decent housing and a suitable environment. Even so, this goal expresses both a moral and legal basis for possible public policies related to rental housing. In fact, many subsequent laws affecting housing refer to it as their justification.[2] Because of the unequal distribution of incomes and wealth in the United States and the high cost of "decent" housing, attaining this goal implies redistributing at least some resources to the poor.

Rental housing is also greatly affected by many local, state, and federal policies and programs not primarily aimed at housing. Accounting for the many goals of all these policies relevant to rental housing would be overwhelmingly complicated. I have therefore condensed all such goals into four major objectives, two affecting supply and two affecting

This chapter is taken from Anthony Downs, *Rental Housing in the 1980s* (Brookings Institution: Washington, D.C., 1983).

*The Brookings Institution, Washington, D.C.

demand. The supply objectives are stimulating the production of new rental housing and making more intensive use of existing structures as rental housing. The second includes encouraging (1) proper maintenance of existing rental housing units; (2) conversion of nonresidential structures into rental units; (3) return of retrievable units to current rental use; (4) division of large single-family units into two or more units, some used for rental; and (5) continued use, rather than removal, of rental units now in the active inventory.

The first demand objective is helping poor renters by enabling those now living in substandard housing to occupy better units or by providing financial aid to those who pay excessive fractions of their income for rent, including many who already occupy decent units. (The latter really suffer from inadequate income rather than inadequate housing.) The second objective is encouraging homeownership among all income groups. This is relevant to rental housing markets because implementing it tends to shift households from renting to owning their homes.

The Tension Between Supply and Demand Objectives

Achieving both supply objectives requires improving the profitability of rental housing, which in turn requires raising rents substantially. Developers are not building many new unsubsidized rental units, and financial institutions are not funding many, because rents are not high enough in relation to construction and operating costs to make doing so profitable. Similarly, many owners of existing rental units are converting them to condominiums because it is much more profitable to sell them than to continue renting them. Other owners are allowing their rental properties to deteriorate because spending the money to maintain them is not justified by the added profits gained. Furthermore, non-new rental units will not be added to the inventory unless they promise profitability, and substantial numbers of non-new units must be created in the 1980s if major rental shortfalls are to be avoided.

To make rental housing profitable enough to call forth an adequate future supply, rents will have to increase for at least several years much faster than operating costs, building costs, the general price level, or consumer incomes—reversing the trend prevailing from 1960 to 1981.[3] Only in that way can enough revenues be generated to justify the investments required to create additional new and non-new units and to maintain and operate existing units. The only alternative is a massive infusion of government subsidies, which seems unlikely in the present political and budgetary climate.

Undoubtedly, such rent escalation would be bitterly opposed by most tenants and would be especially onerous for poor tenants. Rapidly rising rents would make achievement of the first demand objective much more difficult because the cost of helping poor renters occupy decent housing would increase accordingly. That would reduce the number of households that could be effectively aided with any given amount of subsidy, or it would decrease the effectiveness of any given subsidy distributed to all needy households.

Thus there is a fundamental tension between the two supply objectives and the first demand objective. This tension makes it difficult to formulate any set of public policies concerning rental housing that will be both balanced and effective. The supply must be increased greatly to meet future needs, and that requires raising the price (rents). Yet raising the price worsens the situation of low-income renters and increases the public subsidy costs of assisting them.

This underlying tension makes it hard to formulate policies on rental housing that have a real chance of being adopted. The number of people whose short-run welfare would be reduced by higher rents is vastly greater than the number who would gain from them. In 1979, 63.3 million persons were renting 27.2 million units from their owners. I estimate that a maximum of 12.6 million other persons owned those units (see table 2.1), and the correct number may be much smaller.[4] At least twice as many households contain tenants as contain landlords, and the number of tenants is five times the number of landlords. Elected

Table 2.1
Ownership of Rental Housing Units, 1979

Type	Number of units (thousands)	Estimated average units per separate owner	Number of owners (thousands)
Single-family units	8,390	1.0	8,390
Multifamily structures			
2–4 units	7,475	2.5	2,990
5–19 units	6,100	7.5	813
20–49 units	2,082	30.0	69
50 or more units	2,442	55.0	44
Mobile homes	671	2.0	336
Total	27,160	2.1	12,933

Source: U.S. Department of Housing and Urban Development and Bureau of the Census, *Annual Housing Survey, 1979, Part C* U.S. Government Printing Office, 1980), p. 4, and author's estimates.

officials are thus likely to be more sensitive to the demands of tenants than of rental owners, especially in areas where tenants are heavily concentrated.

Renters compose over 70 percent of the residents of New York City and over 80 percent of the residents of Santa Monica, California. It is not surprising that both cities have stringent rent controls. Nonetheless, many cities do not have such laws. Perhaps the relatively widespread ownership of rental housing compared with other forms of wealth in our society (such as stocks and bonds or small businesses) makes local governments more sensitive to the drawbacks of rent controls than sheer numbers would indicate was likely.

The Importance of Federal Policies

Because the federal government is uniquely able to influence the flow of capital and the distribution of income nationwide, a broad range of federal policies on interest rates, taxes, access to credit markets, and subsidies to the poor profoundly affect housing markets. Until recently, these policies created a sheltered position for housing within the economy, and many argue that this sheltered position should be restored. This section examines a variety of federal policies that influence rental housing; subsequent sections consider the limitations of federal policies and recommend specific policy changes.

Interest Rates

Federal monetary policies profoundly influence the economic feasibility of building new rental units and selling, modernizing, or refinancing existing ones. Throughout 1981 and well into 1982 very high real and nominal interest rates severely constrained all types of mortgage lending. That constraint depressed both the building of new rental units and transactions concerning existing ones. These high interest rates were caused by a combination of continuing inflation, strictures on the growth of the money supply by the Federal Reserve, and fears of large future federal deficits.

There is great disagreement among economists about how to lower nominal and real interest rates in the long run. I cannot resolve this issue here, but, assuming there is *some way* to reduce interest rates, I would like to look at the implications for rental housing.

Lower interest rates would greatly improve the profitability of building, buying and operating, or refinancing rental housing. For example, a 21.9 percent fall in mortgage interest rates from 16.0 percent to 12.5 percent with constant rents would raise the market value sustainable from a given property by 24.6 percent.[5]

For real estate activity to return to the level normal before 1980, nominal mortgage interest rates would have to fall from early-1982 levels of about 16–17 percent to about 12–13 percent. But even that level of activity would not add much new rental housing. That result would probably require further declines in nominal mortgage rates to around 8 or 9 percent—though no one knows for certain. Thus reducing interest rates in both real and nominal terms is a necessary but not sufficient step to constructing any large number of new rental units.

Credit Markets and Taxes

From 1945 to about 1980 federal credit and tax policies made investing in housing—especially owner-occupied housing—more advantageous than investing in most other widely available assets, such as stocks, bonds, and businesses. Housing's advantages sprang from federal regulations that sheltered mortgage lending in the nation's credit markets and from federal tax benefits that accrued to homeowners. In addition to aiding builders, realtors, and households buying homes, these advantages undoubtedly made the overall flow of financial capital into housing much larger than it would otherwise have been.

Federal regulations protected thrift institutions (savings and loan associations and mutual savings banks) from having to pay full market prices to obtain deposits from small-scale savers. Thrifts were created to borrow money for short terms, mainly as savings deposits, and lend it as long-term home mortgages so as to encourage construction and purchase of owner-occupied housing. For the thrifts to be economically viable, short-term interest rates had to remain lower than long-term rates most of the time. To strengthen that viability, Congress put ceilings on the rates thrift institutions and banks could pay for savings deposits and allowed thrifts to pay slightly higher rates than banks. In return, thrifts had to use most of their loanable funds for home mortgages.

This arrangement often reduced mortgage rates below what they would otherwise have been, especially during tight money periods. Lower mortgage rates made it easier for people to buy homes and to buy or develop rental properties. This strategy worked so well that thrifts were the largest source of home mortgage finance from 1950 to 1978.[6]

In addition, households that bought their own homes enjoyed tax benefits not easily obtainable from other investments. These benefits, combined with unanticipated inflation, encouraged people to invest in their own homes rather than in corporate equities, bonds, or unincorporated businesses.

Housing's sheltered financial position was ended in the late 1970s and early 1980s by a combination of inflation and changes in federal regulations. Inflation drove general interest rates above the ceilings for savings rates for much longer periods than previously. Also, regulatory changes allowed small-scale savers to invest in new forms of savings without rate ceilings, such as money market funds. Many savers withdrew their funds from thrift institutions because they could get higher returns elsewhere. To defend thrifts, federal regulators gradually raised the ceilings for savings rates, which helped thrifts slow outflows but also raised their costs. Because most thrifts still held large portfolios of older long-term mortgages paying low yields, their average cost of retaining deposits rose above their average yield on assets. As a result, most thrifts lost money in 1981 and 1982. Their basic strategy—borrowing short and lending long—had been made unviable because short-term rates had risen well above both current and earlier long-term rates.[7] Unless this new relationship among rates for investments of different durations changes, thrifts can no longer finance housing in the traditional way.

Moreover, the relative tax advantages of investing in homeownership were greatly reduced by the Economic Recovery Tax Act of 1981, which increased the tax benefits available from other types of investments. Thus both major forms of favorable investment treatment enjoyed by housing investments in the 1970s were notably diminished in 1980–1981.

Some people argue that housing should be returned to a sheltered position in the nation's financial structure. Then thrifts could again make mortgage loans at lower rates than would prevail otherwise. However, any such arrangement requires either that people who save in thrifts receive lower returns than they could find elsewhere or that the government make up the difference with a subsidy. But savers will not accept lower returns voluntarily. In fact, one reason monetary authorities ended housing's sheltered position was to help small savers receive market rates. Therefore, the only politically acceptable way to restore housing's sheltered position is through a federal subsidy to savers in thrift institutions.

Congress passed one such subsidy in 1981 by allowing thrift and bank depositors to receive a limited amount of interest free from federal income taxes. This privilege lasted only one year to help thrifts escape from the squeeze on their earnings described above. However, this subsidy did not remedy the cause of that squeeze: low earnings on thrifts' large portfolio of older mortgages combined with prolonged periods when short-term rates exceed long-term rates. Also, if this tax-free feature lasted only one year, it would not permanently restore housing's sheltered financial position.

A permanent restoration would encourage larger flows of credit into housing. But more credit would not necessarily increase production of new or even non-new housing units.[8] Wherever local restrictions make building more housing difficult, easier credit availability combined with strong local demand tends to drive up prices of the existing inventory. In California, for example, the median sales price of existing single-family homes rose over 21 percent a year from 1976 to 1980.[9] Moreover, investment in housing was already encouraged by its many tax advantages before tax-free savings were available. These tax advantages distorted the allocation of capital that would have occurred if tax benefits for other investments had been equal to those for housing. The recent extension of greater tax benefits to other investments may therefore actually reduce overall distortions in capital allocation, rather than increasing them.

Restoring the favored financial treatment of housing would have the disadvantages of continuing to distort investment decisions and using scarce federal dollars to aid nonpoor mortgage borrowers and high-bracket homeowners while aid to the poor is being cut. Hence this policy is basically undesirable. If short-term interest rates remain high very long, some federal assistance for thrift institutions will be necessary to prevent their collapse. But it need not involve restoring housing's sheltered position in credit markets or its great tax advantages compared with other investments.

Subsidies to Poor Renters

The federal government is a better source of funds for policies that redistribute income than either state or local governments. In fact, it already provides subsidies to a significant fraction of all poor renters in the United States.[10] At the same time it provides much larger implicit subsidies to homeowners who deduct their mortgage interest payments and local property taxes from their federally taxable income. Subsidizing the poor, by definition, requires government to tax affluent households more than poor ones, to aim its spending more at the poor than at affluent households, or to do both. But many relatively affluent citizens taxed heavily by a local government can move to nearby communities that do not tax them as much. Moreover, they can do so without having to change jobs or sacrifice their access to the entire area. Hence, if a local government tries to carry out major income redistribution, it may drive many of its more affluent citizens beyond its taxing jurisdiction.

State governments confront the same problem. Because many major U.S. metropolitan areas contain parts of several states, residents of one state can move to another nearby without having to leave their economic area. The recent burgeoning of luxury homes and corporate headquarters in southern Connecticut was generated in precisely this way by high taxes in New York. But it is difficult to move out of the United States altogether to escape redistributive federal fiscal policies. So public policies aimed at helping poor renters (the first demand objective) should be funded by the federal government, although they can sometimes be effectively administered by state or local governments.

Housing Markets

Another crucial federal role is to reduce obstacles that local governments deliberately erect to the efficient and equitable operation of housing markets. Many suburban communities of middle- and upper-income households do not want poor households as neighbors. One reason is fear that property values might decline as a result. Residents use their political dominance of local governments to pass exclusionary laws, such as zoning regulations, building codes, and subdivision ordinances that require dwellings too expensive for most low- and moderate-income households. Many communities also drastically limit the amount of multifamily rental housing within their borders. This limitation and high land costs raise the rents there beyond what low- and moderate-income households can pay. Such interference with housing markets is not accidental; rather, it is one of the central purposes of many suburban governments.

Some regulation of housing and neighborhood quality is undoubtedly desirable to eliminate inefficient conflicts over land use and to prevent unhealthful substandard conditions. But the regulations adopted by many suburban communities go beyond what is necessary to achieve these reasonable goals. By helping to cause disproportionate concentrations of high-income and low-income residents within different parts of metropolitan areas, exclusionary regulations often produce both inequitable and inefficient patterns of land use.[11]

Another market intervention undesirable in the long run is local rent controls. They are usually adopted only in communities where middle-income renters form a large part of the electorate. However, the short-run beneficiaries of rent controls include low- and moderate-income renters, too. The persons treated inequitably by rent controls are the owners of controlled properties, who are deprived of competitive returns on their investments. Rent controls also have a variety of disadvantages in the long run.

They reduce the quality of housing services provided to tenants of controlled units because owners cut back on maintenance.

They cut off additions to the rental housing supply and thereby generate shortages.

They increase property tax burdens on owner-occupants because the assessed values of rental units decline as a result of deterioration.

They increase the costs of owner-occupied housing by shifting rental demand to ownership units.

They somewhat restrict the mobility of renters if moving requires them to give up units with very low controlled rents.[12]

Both exclusionary zoning and rent controls are thus inefficient and inequitable interferences with overall urban housing markets. Both have undesirable impacts not confined to the communities adopting them, but harmful to their overall metropolitan areas. Yet certain local communities adopt them because of the parochial composition of their electorates, compared with the composition of society at large. Politically dominant groups within those communities benefit from such policies, but do not have to pay the social costs. Those costs are borne mainly by people living elsewhere (as with exclusionary zoning) or by groups within the community who are opposed to such interferences (as with rent controls). Local governments in these communities are not likely to sacrifice the benefits most of their residents are receiving in order to aid their metropolitan area as a whole. Only a government with jurisdiction over an entire metropolitan area is likely to have an appropriate perspective on the housing needs of all area residents. Except for the very few metropolitan governments within the United States, only the state and federal governments normally have such broad jurisdictions.

The breadth of federal jurisdiction is a particular advantage in regard to rent controls. Although state governments could also prohibit rent controls, a federal prohibition would be more effective than state actions within metropolitan areas that encompass parts of several states. Furthermore, only federal prohibition of rent controls is likely to convince potential investors in rental housing that the profitability of their investments would not be jeopardized by future actions of individual state or local governments.

The Limitations of Federal Policies

There are major disadvantages to having decisions on local land use made by governments with broad jurisdictions, especially the federal government. The immense diversity of local urban conditions, even within individual metropolitan areas, can rarely be accommodated by distant state and federal governments. Their remote influence is usually effective only in developing rules that can be clearly applied in many different local circumstances. Given the complexity and variety of exclusionary land use practices, it is difficult for the federal government to reduce or inhibit such practices. In contrast, it could very simply influence local rent controls by prohibiting them altogether. That is why I do not believe federal prohibition of rent controls would constitute unwarranted interference in the complexities of local conditions.

Regardless of whether federal interference in local housing markets is desirable, the constitutional separation of state and federal powers makes it legally difficult. The federal government cannot mandate changes over which it has no constitutional authority, and local governments are under the constitutional authority of the states. Federal influence on local regulations is likely to be most effective when accompanied by some large federally funded incentive for local governments to follow federal suggestions.

One such incentive is a believable threat to reduce existing federal financial aid to local governments if those suggestions are not heeded. Many suburbs engaging in exclusionary zoning do not receive much federal financial aid; their behavior would not be swayed by such threats. But urban communities most likely to adopt rent controls often depend heavily on federal funds for fiscal support; they would be quite susceptible to federal financial pressure to prohibit or abolish rent controls. Even if those incentives were not effective, the federal government could devise other ways to make most rental units free from local controls, if Congress were willing to pass them. Congress could, for example, exempt from local rent controls all housing units financed by agencies insured or regulated by the federal government.

Desirable Federal Policies

In addition to helping establish an appropriate overall economic climate, the federal government should perform two principal roles concerning rental housing: (1) helping to reduce the poverty of low-income renters and (2) preventing local governments from adopting rent controls. These roles and the policies they imply are outlined here.

Subsidies to Poor Renters

Millions of people throughout the United States have such low income they cannot afford dwelling units with the minimum size and quality regarded as necessary by prevailing middle-class standards. Many would be able to solve their housing problems without subsidies if the overall economy grew more rapidly than it has in the early 1980s, because they could get jobs or increase their earnings. But even sustained prosperity would not eliminate poverty altogether, as experience in the 1960s and early 1970s proves.[13] Enabling all or even most poor households to live in decent dwellings therefore requires providing many with subsidies.

Like most economists, I believe the best way to do that would be for the federal government to provide the poor with jobs or greater direct income assistance. However, this approach faces political obstacles. Congress has been unwilling to fund enough direct aid to eradicate poverty, assuming that would be possible.[14] It prefers aiding the poor through various types of in-kind assistance, such as food stamps and medicare, tied to the consumption of specific goods or services. Such "earmarked" assistance has the practical advantage of attracting political support from providers of the goods or services concerned. A similar approach could be taken in the case of housing through a nationwide housing voucher program like the one tested in the experimental housing allowance program.[15] Therefore, if Congress remains unwilling to provide more direct aid, I recommend making housing vouchers available to all renting households with income below 50 percent of the areawide median.[16] Based on experience in the experimental housing allowance program, only about half of all eligible households would actually participate in such a program.[17]

This program could be paid for without any net increase in federal spending by modestly reducing the present tax benefits received by homeowners. The Congressional Budget Office (CBO) estimated that homeowners saved $36 billion in federal taxes in fiscal 1982 by deducting mortgage interest and property taxes from their taxable income.[18] CBO calculated that this saving would rise to $53.1 billion by fiscal 1984. In contrast, the total outlays for a full-scale housing voucher entitlement program would probably rise to about $7.3 billion in fiscal 1984.[19] Reducing estimated homeowner tax benefits by only about 14 percent would completely offset the cost of such a program in 1984.

I believe this could best be done by converting homeowners' present tax deductibility benefits to a tax credit and then reducing the rate used to compute that credit enough to pay for the voucher program. CBO estimated that a tax credit of about 25 percent of homeowners' mortgage interest and property tax payments would have produced the same total revenues as current deductions in 1982. But it would yield $7.9 billion more revenues by fiscal 1986. Hence it might be possible to finance a nationwide housing voucher program for poor renters with no net increase in federal costs and without much reduction in the tax credit rate below 25 percent.

Moreover, a tax credit is much fairer than a tax deduction. A credit provides every taxpayer the same amount of tax savings for each dollar of mortgage interest payment or property tax, regardless of the taxpayer's marginal tax rate. In contrast, a deduction provides much greater tax savings to wealthier taxpayers who are in higher marginal tax brackets. This fact alone justifies changing homeowner benefits to a tax credit, whether or not a housing voucher program is adopted.

The Reagan administration has already advocated shifting most federal low-income housing assistance to a housing voucher program.[20] But it also suggested scaling down current funding for such assistance, while leaving homeowners' vastly larger tax benefits intact. The approach I recommend would create a more equitable distribution of federal housing benefits by shifting some from high-income to low-income households. Yet it would still provide immense tax advantages to owner-occupants, thereby continuing to encourage homeownership.

Prohibition of Rent Controls

A nationwide prohibition of rent controls, or the creation of extremely strong federal incentives for local governments to abstain from such controls, would remove a major obstacle to investment in rental housing by private developers and capital suppliers. However, such a prohibition should not be adopted unless it is accompanied by some form of increased financial assistance to low-income renters, such as the housing voucher program described earlier. Added assistance will be necessary to protect them from big rent increases. Housing is by far the largest single expense for most poor households. In 1979 the median fraction of income paid for gross rent was 26 percent for all renters, but over 60 percent for renters with income below $3,000, 44 percent for those with income from $3,000 to $6,999, and 31 percent for those with income from $7,000 to $9,999.[21] It would clearly be inequitable to impose relatively heavy financial burdens on many of the poorest households in order to encourage private developers to add to the overall supply of rental housing. Such encouragement could be achieved without this inequity if a federal prohibition of rent controls were coupled with increased financial assistance to poor renters.

Other Policies

Certain other federal policies concerning rental housing are desirable but should have much lower priority. These include (1) providing some rehabilitation assistance to owners of deteriorated rental units; (2) allowing state housing finance agencies to continue using tax-exempt bonds to finance new construction of rental housing under certain limited circumstances; (3) building a small number of new public housing units each year to meet specialized needs not served by the private market; and (4) turning over surplus units foreclosed by the Federal Housing Administration to local governments or local public housing authorities at nominal cost.

The federal government should definitely *not* adopt certain other policies. These include (1) directly subsidizing construction of new rental units for middle-income households; (2) creating new tax deductions for renters; (3) selling off existing public housing projects to private owners; (4) providing tax benefits to developers or owners of rental housing beyond those already adopted in the Economic Recovery Tax Act of 1981; and (5) creating special housing voucher programs only for occupants of public housing or of units undergoing condominium conversion.

The Future of Rental Housing

Privately furnished rental units now vastly outnumber publicly furnished ones in the United States. But coming rapid rent increases in private units could change this balance drastically over the next decade or two, as has happened in Great Britain since 1945. The remainder of this chapter discusses this possibility and relates it to the policies I have recommended.

Rapid rent increases in the near future will make poor households worse off in real terms, if no further government actions are taken to assist them. As rents rise, many injured households will pressure governments to help them. Possible government reactions include local adoption of rent controls and federal provision of various subsidies. But federal officials are now disinclined to expand aid to the poor; in fact, they are substantially reducing such aid in real terms. Hence local controls will be the only immediate public policy response to higher rents that seems both politically and economically feasible.

Rent controls will undoubtedly benefit poor households and many nonpoor ones in the short run. Therefore, powerful political pressures favoring such controls will appear in many cities. These pressures will cause more widespread adoption of rent controls unless the federal government prevents it.

Even if a minority of large cities adopts rent controls, enough might do so to alter the nation's rental housing supply in the long run because the longer rent controls remain in force, the more difficult it is to get rid of them. The gap between existing rents and those needed to make construction of new rental units economically feasible rises continuously while controls are in force, and shortages of rental housing develop or intensify. Sudden removal of controls generates a rapid increase in rents, causing substantial hardships for many poor households. Yet the private sector does not respond by immediately building many new rental units; that occurs only after rents have risen enough to make it feasible. Thus, right after controls are ended, renters suffer added hardships with no result except the enrichment of landlords. To avoid that unpopular outcome, elected officials are tempted to keep rent controls in force. This is the case in New York City today.

Yet the continuation of rent controls only increases the shortage of rental housing and the deterioration of the existing rental inventory. If these ills became widespread, they would eventually generate strong pressures for the federal government to do something about them. By then, rent controls would have been in operation for several years in many markets and would influence the form of federal policy responses. It may then be politically difficult to abolish controls completely so that rents can rise rapidly to the level at which private developers will build more rental units. It may be equally difficult to use housing vouchers to support the low-income rental market, because vouchers do not work well under rent controls.[22] The federal government may be pressured into aiding the poor by expanding the supply of new subsidized housing. This is especially likely if current attitudes against federal aid to the poor have changed, as such intangible moods typically do in time.

Yet building subsidized housing is the costliest way to improve the poor's housing. It would also reduce the relative importance of the private rental sector in housing markets. This is precisely what has happened in several European nations: private rental housing has shrunk dramatically, and public housing has greatly expanded. Ironically, this eventual result of the nation's present conservative mood would generate conditions highly inconsistent with that mood.

Of course, initially failing to prohibit rent controls or adopt additional financial aid to poor renters would not inexorably lead to massive expansion of publicly subsidized housing. Yet this scenario is quite plausible, even though most households at every income level prefer living in privately owned quarters to living in public housing. At the very least, such a scenario shows that decisions on the amount and nature of federal housing subsidies and other aids to the poor are closely related to decisions on local rent controls. Both types of decisions have vital implications for "the realization as soon as feasible of . . . a decent home and a suitable living arrangement for every American family."

Notes

1. *Basic Laws and Authorities on Housing and Community Development, Revised through January 3, 1979,* Committee Print, House Committee on Banking, Finance, and Urban Affairs, 94 Cong. 1 sess. (U.S. Government Printing Office, 1979), p. 1.

2. Congress has established several other primary objectives for housing policy as means of pursuing the basic goal stated above. These are the following.

Providing housing assistance to low-income households. This includes enabling those now living in substandard or overcrowded housing to occupy decent units and financially aiding those who now pay very high fractions of their income to live in decent units. *Low-income households* are usually defined as those with annual income less than 80 percent of the median household income in the area concerned. This definition is used to establish eligibility for the Section 8 housing subsidy program. Because 80 percent of the median household income is now about double the poverty-level income, this definition includes many households with incomes well above the official poverty level. Hence the term *very low income* is sometimes applied to households with income below 50 percent of the median household income in the area. The term *moderate income* was initially used in the Housing Act of 1968, applying to households with income between the very low income and low-income levels as defined above. Therefore, the goal of serving moderate-income households can be considered as encompassed within the goal of serving low-income households, as they are now defined.

Encouraging homeownership among households at all income levels.

Stimulating the economy by increasing activity in the housing industry.

Increasing the total available supply of decent housing units.

Improving the quality of deteriorated neighborhoods.

Providing housing assistance to numerous specific groups, such as the elderly, Indians, and persons displaced by government actions. The assistance is the same as described above concerning low-income households.

Congress has also adopted several other housing goals I consider secondary because of the lesser emphasis they have received. These include providing housing assistance to colleges, stabilizing annual housing output at a high level, encouraging housing innovations, creating employment and training opportunities for residents of low-income areas, encouraging maximum feasible participation of private enterprise and capital in meeting housing needs, and achieving reduced concentration of low-income households in deteriorated urban neighborhoods. This list of goals is taken from Anthony Downs, *Federal Housing Subsidies: How Are They Working?* (Lexington Books, 1973), pp. 1–2.

3. From July 1981 to December 1982, the consumer price index component for residential rent rose faster than the overall index; *Economic Report of the President, January 1983,* p. 221. Hence this change has already begun.

4. My estimate of the average number of units held by each owner is a conservative one; if the average is in fact higher, the number of separate owners would be smaller than my estimate.

5. These results were derived from a model that assumes a down-payment ratio of 0.25, an operating-cost ratio of 0.41, a debt-service ratio of 1.25, a depreciable life of twenty-five years, a marginal tax rate of 0.5, and monthly rent of $245. However, the precise value of these variables is not critical, as long as they remain the same when interest rates are changed. The model is presented in Chapter 7 of Anthony Downs, *Rental Housing in the 1980s* (Brookings Institution: Washington, D.C., 1983).

6. *Federal Reserve Bulletin*, 1950–81.

7. The original strategy cannot work as long as the blended average rate from both current and past mortgages in the thrift industry's total portfolio is below the average current rate it must pay for savings and other deposits.

8. For a discussion of this point, see chapter 3 of Anthony Downs, *Rental Housing in the 1980s* (Brookings Institution: Washington, D.C., 1983), and Anthony Downs, "Are We Using Too Much Capital for Financing Housing?" in Federal National Mortgage Association, *Housing Finance in the Eighties: Issues and Options* (Washington, D.C.: FNMA, May 1981), pp. 66–79.

9. California Association of Realtors, *California Real Estate Trends Newsletter*, vol. 2 (April 10, 1981), p. 1. The median price rose from $44,800 in February 1976 to $97,481 in February 1980, or at a compound annual rate of 21.5 percent. In the following year, it rose only 6.0 percent, however.

10. Jill Khadduri and Raymond J. Struyk estimated that about one-third of all renter households with incomes below 50 percent of their area median income were receiving federal housing subsidies of some type as of 1981. See Jill Khadduri and Raymond J. Struyk, *Housing Vouchers: From Here to Entitlement?* (Urban Institute, 1980), pp. 3–5.

11. For a discussion of this point, see Anthony Downs, *Neighborhoods and Urban Development* (Brookings Institution, 1981), chap. 4. See also *The Report of the President's Commission on Housing* (GPO, 1982), pp. 199–222.

12. This is most likely if the ordinance concerned allows landlords to raise rents without limit whenever units are voluntarily vacated.

13. The fraction of U.S. citizens with money income below the official poverty line fell from 22.4 percent in 1959 to 11.1 percent in 1973, but has remained above the latter level ever since. Taking in-kind transfer payments into account, the fraction of citizens with real income below the official poverty level has probably fallen as low as 6–7 percent. Much of this decline, however, must be attributed to government transfer programs, rather than improved earnings from the private sector. See Laurence E. Lynn, Jr., "A Decade of Policy Developments in the Income Maintenance System," in Robert H. Haveman, ed., *A Decade of Federal Antipoverty Programs: Achievements, Failures, and Lessons* (Academic Press, 1977), pp. 88–102; Felicity Skidmore, "Progress Against Poverty: Summary and Outlook for the Future," in Robert D. Plotnick and Felicity Skidmore, *Progress Against Poverty: A Review of the 1964–1974 Decade* (Academic Press, 1977), pp. 169–79; Morton Paglin, "Poverty in the United States: A Reevaluation," *Policy Review*, no. 8 (Spring 1979), pp. 7–24; and James R. Storey, "Income Security," in John L. Palmer and Isabel V. Sawhill, ed., *The Reagan Experiment* (Urban Institute Press, 1982), p. 371. See also Bureau of the Census, *Statistical Abstract of the United States, 1980* (GPO, 1980), p. 465.

14. Poverty probably could be fully eliminated through public policies if it is defined as *income poverty*, that is, poverty that results from a combined money and in-kind income below some officially established level. But poverty almost certainly could not be fully eliminated through public action if it is defined as also encompassing certain personal attitudes and behavior patterns.

15. For an analysis of the experimental housing allowance program and its effectiveness, see Katharine L. Bradbury and Anthony Downs, eds., *Do Housing Allowances Work?* (Brookings Institution, 1981).

16. For a discussion of the possible form and costs of such a program, see Khadduri and Struyk, *Housing Vouchers*.

17. See Bradbury and Downs, *Housing Allowances*, pp. 21–27, 113–45.

18. Congressional Budget Office, *The Tax Treatment of Homeownership: Issues and Options* (CBO, 1981), p. 7. Homeowners' ability to deduct mortgage interest and property taxes from their taxable income does not constitute a true subsidy, relative to other investments. All investors (except those buying tax-exempt bonds) can deduct interest and other expenses from their taxable incomes. But other investors must also pay income taxes on the net income from their investments, whereas homeowners are free from that obligation. Homeowners do not earn cash income on their homes because they rent those homes themselves. But the imputed rents they receive constitute "real" income to them as investors, on which they do not have to pay income taxes. This freedom from tax liability is a true subsidy not available to investors in stocks, bonds, or other investments. The exact size of the resulting benefit for homeowners is hard to measure because of uncertainty about what the level of imputed rents should

be, in the absence of a freely operating market, though there is a market for rental of single-family homes. But past measurement efforts indicate this benefit is at least as large as the tax savings received from deducting both mortgage interest and property taxes from taxable income. Therefore, I have used calculations concerning those tax savings as a surrogate for the true subsidy to homeowners in this part of the analysis. For estimates comparing this surrogate to the true subsidy, see Henry Aaron, *Shelter and Subsidies* (Brookings Institution, 1972), p. 56.

19. Khadduri and Struyk, *Housing Vouchers*, p. 21.

20. Department of Housing and Urban Development. *Fiscal Year 1983 Budget: Summary* (GPO, February 1982), pp. H-2–H-5.

21. U.S. Department of Housing and Urban Development and Bureau of the Census, *Annual Housing Survey, 1979, Part C* (GPO, 1981), p. 7. The fractions of total expenditures devoted to housing by very poor households are somewhat lower than these percentages, since such households typically spend more than their current income. I am indebted to Henry Aaron for pointing this out.

22. Controls prevent owners from meeting the full costs of operation, even if vouchers permit poor tenants to pay allowable rents without undue hardship. Hence units deteriorate and shortages arise in the long run, in spite of vouchers.

3

The Future of Rental Housing in California

*Ira S. Lowry**

My main mission is to suggest a frame of reference for discussion of rental housing prospects and policies. I want to remind you of some basic facts about California's current housing circumstances, facts too often ignored in public discussion of housing problems; and to remind you how housing markets work, offering a conceptual framework that will aid clear and consistent thinking about housing issues.

Renters and Their Housing Circumstances, 1970–1985

The most recent comprehensive statistical account of California's housing circumstances is the 1980 Census of Housing, now five years out-of-date.[1] Since 1980 local market conditions in many parts of the state have changed substantially, but the characteristics of the housing stock, its occupants, and their tenure arrangements have changed only marginally.

The Rental Inventory

In 1980 California had 9.2 million habitable year-round dwellings for a population of 23.7 million persons, or one dwelling for every 2.6 persons. About 62 percent of these dwellings were detached single-

---

*Housing and Development consultant.

family houses, (including mobile homes), 14 percent were small multiple dwellings, and 24 percent were in structures containing five or more dwellings. At the time of the census enumeration, 8.6 million of these dwellings were occupied, leaving 577,000 dwellings, or about 6 percent of the stock vacant. Among the occupants, 56 percent were owners and 44 percent were renters.

Although most owners occupy single-family houses and most renters occupy multiple dwellings, there is no necessary correspondence between tenure and type of structure. In California 27 percent of all renters live in detached single-family houses, and nearly half live in structures containing fewer than five dwellings. Single-family houses are rarely built with the intention of operating them as rental properties, but they are often converted to rental use because their owners do not want to live in them and current market conditions are not propitious for selling. Tenure in multiple dwellings is also changeable. For example, during the past decade many apartment buildings have been converted from rentals to condominiums; and in many condominiums one-third or more of the units are currently occupied by renters.

The point of these comments is that the boundary between the rental and owner-occupied inventories is quite flexible, with existing dwellings moving back and forth across that line depending on the property-owner's circumstances and current market conditions. The rental inventory can expand or contract quickly and substantially without new rental construction or demolition.

Housing Quality

Renter-occupied dwellings run the gamut of quality from spacious apartments in luxurious buildings on Wilshire Boulevard to dilapidated stucco boxes in the weed patches of the Central Valley. On average, rented dwellings are slightly older than owner-occupied homes; even so, fully half of the rental inventory was less than twenty years old in 1980, and only 17 percent predated World War II. Renter-occupied dwellings averaged 1.7 bedrooms and 1.2 bathrooms, as compared with the owner-occupied average of 2.8 bedrooms and 1.6 bathrooms. Virtually all renter-occupied dwellings had complete bath and kitchen facilities, electrical service, and some form of space heating.

In addition to being slightly older and substantially smaller than owner-occupied dwellings, rental dwellings tend to be less well maintained. Cosmetics aside, perhaps half of all renter-occupied dwellings would fail a rigorous housing code inspection, as compared with perhaps 40 percent of all owner-occupied dwellings. That estimate does not imply that half the rental stock should be replaced or even that it needs major repairs. Most code violations—hazards to the health and safety of the occupants—could be easily and cheaply corrected by either the occupants or their landlords without the help of home-repair contractors. We should not be misled by the horrible examples that are beloved of the press—they exist, but they are rare.

The current physical condition of a renter-occupied dwelling depends on three factors: its original structural quality; the amount of damage it has since suffered from time, weather, and the occupants; and the maintenance policies that have been pursued by both the landlord and his tenants. Because building codes have been well enforced in California for many years, the original structural quality of nearly all rental housing in the current inventory was at least adequate by code standards. But the tenant-landlord relationship is all too often a vicious circle that leads to careless or even malicious damage by tenants and neglect by landlords of maintenance and repairs. Absent a cooperative and mutually supportive landlord-tenant relationship, neither rehabilitating existing dwellings nor building new ones will yield well-maintained dwellings. This reminder applies alike to privately and publicly owned rental housing.

Availability of Rental Housing

During the 1970s the number of renter-occupied dwellings in California increased by 28 percent, from 3.0 million to 3.8 million. By definition, the number of renter households increased identically. The rental vacancy rate, as measured by the Bureau of the Census, decreased in the San Francisco Bay and South Coast regions of the state but rose sharply in the Central Valley and elsewhere in California. Statewide, the Bureau's rental vacancy rate was 5.7 percent in 1970 and 5.1 percent in 1980.

Although low rental vacancy rates are universally used to justify public regulation of rental housing and subsidies for rental construction, a low vacancy rate does not signify a housing shortage, and a high vacancy rate does not signify a surplus in any sense that is meaningful for public policy.

For example, during the 1970s our housing inventory grew most rapidly in those parts of the state where vacancy rates were highest. These were also the areas with the most rapid growth in population and the most rapid rates of household formation. The reason is that builders anticipated such growth, and the consequent rapid inventory expansion resulted in a rolling backlog of vacancies. In areas where population is static, building activity is minimal and the inhabitants settle into the available inventory, achieving a high inventory utilization rate that is undisturbed by inventory change. On the other hand, in an area whose population is declining, vacancy rates may be high because superfluous dwellings are only slowly withdrawn from the market.

The concept of a housing shortage is necessarily relative to some standard. Because there are always as many renter-occupied dwellings as there are renter households, counting houses and households is not an appropriate methodology; nor for the reasons just given, do vacancy rates equate with shortages. I have suggested elsewhere that the appropriate tests are the trends in real housing consumption per household and per capita. I concluded that from 1970 to 1980 rental housing consumption in California increased by 6 percent per renter household and 8 percent per capita. I was unable to reconcile that finding with contemporary claims of a serious rental housing shortage: The supply was clearly at least as abundant, relative to the renter population, in 1980 as in 1970.[2]

Rents and the Ability to Pay

Shortage or surplus, there is no quarreling with the observation that rents have skyrocketed since 1970. From 1970 to 1975 the average annual increase in gross rent was 5.6 percent; from 1975 to 1980, 10.4 percent; and from 1980 to 1985, probably about 9 percent. Cumulatively, my index of residential rents for California indicate that the market price of a fixed quantity of rental housing service more than tripled during the fifteen years, 1970 to 1985.[3]

However, the social impact of escalating rents should be seen against the backdrop of general inflation in wages and prices. From 1970 to 1980 annual increases in rents were closely matched by increases in the nonhousing components of the California Consumer Price Index and by increases in renters' incomes. Only during the most recent five-year period have rent increases outstripped these other indexes of inflation.

Despite a doubling of rents between 1970 and 1980 and despite the increase in real housing consumption by renters, census data indicate that the average rent/income ratio only rose from 0.32 to 0.33 over the decade; the ratios for the very poor and the elderly actually decreased because their incomes rose more rapidly than rents.[4] The statistical data for that decade offer little support for the view that renters were badly squeezed. I do not have data to extend that analysis to 1980–1985, but I judge that consumption has leveled off and the average rent/income ratio has climbed to about 0.35.

There is a preposterous notion that landlords have some kind of monopoly power in their dealings with tenants. Nothing could be further from the truth. In all but the smallest communities rental housing is an intensely competitive industry. Within a metropolitan area such as Los Angeles, there are thousands of landlords each anxious to keep his units occupied. About one-third of all renters move at least once during a year, and some move more than once. Consequently, roughly 40 percent of all rented dwellings come on the market in the course of a year, offering thousands of alternatives to homeseekers.

Except where they are regulated, landlords no doubt set rents as high as they think the market will bear. Prospective tenants, on the other hand, look for bargains, choosing the most attractive combinations of rent and quality from among many alternatives. Overpriced rentals stay vacant until the landlord reappraises his market and reduces the rent. A landlord's reservation price—the lowest rent he will accept as an alternative to vacancy—depends on his operating cost and the current or expected future market value of his property if used for some other purpose. The rent he can actually get is demand-determined in the short run—reflecting consumers' willingness and ability to pay for housing services.

Many people, especially renters, say that rents in California today are too high. This is true in the sense that tenants would prefer to get the same housing services for less than they actually pay; but neither real rents nor rent/income ratios changed substantially from 1970 to 1980, when such complaints were also common. And according to my calculations, the typical landlord's real net operating income fell by 30 percent from 1970 to 1977. Aided by Proposition 13 and a tighter market after 1977, landlords managed to restore real net operating income to its 1970 level by 1982.[5] I suspect that real net operating income today is 10 to 15 percent higher than it was in 1970.

Prospects for the Future

What can be said about the future? Should we expect the renter population to grow or shrink? Will rents rise more than or less than prices in general?

The Prospective Demand for Rental Housing

As California's population grows, the total demand for housing services will increase. As real incomes rise, the per-capita demand will also increase. However, the division of this demand between the homeowner and rental markets depends on a number of factors that do not easily lend themselves to quantitative a priori analysis.

For most Californians, renting is a transitional housing arrangement, preferred for the interval between leaving the parental home and starting a family of one's own—a period in which residential mobility is high, savings are minimal, income is unreliable, and social life in public places is attractive. When a householder's plans are uncertain, renting rather than owning helps to keep options open.

Later, when a breadwinner settles into a more or less permanent job, marries, and starts a family, homeownership becomes more attractive. Home becomes the focus of life rather than merely a place to sleep, and most people seek the freedom, bestowed by ownership, to rearrange their domestic environments to fit their own standards of comfort and attractiveness. Moreover, rental quarters suitable for raising children (i.e., those with several bedrooms, safe outdoor play space, and good neighborhood schools) are generally hard to find.

In old age a homeowner often chooses to sell his home and return to renting. The house may be inconveniently large once his children have left home. Housekeeping, home repair, and outdoor maintenance, once pleasures, become increasingly burdensome as health and vigor decline. A smaller apartment, maintained by the landlord, relieves an elderly person of domestic chores and responsibilities and of the expense of repairs that will outlive him.

Not everyone goes through this tenure cycle. Those whose incomes are permanently low (because they are unable to work or lack remunerative skills) may not be able to obtain the credit they need to buy a home or may reasonably doubt their ability to carry the costs of ownership year in and year out. Others who could afford homeownership are not attracted by life in a single-family house with lawns to mow and garbage to be carried out. They prefer living in multiple dwellings where landlords are responsible for maintenance, so they can focus their energies on their jobs, hobbies, or social life. At the same time many elderly persons who are financially able to choose between renting and owning are so rooted in their homes and neighborhoods that they stay even at the cost of onerous chores and worries.

Considering tenure choice from this perspective, three demographic trends are particularly salient for California's rental housing markets. One is the changing age-distribution of our adult population; the second is the changing family structure; and the third is the changing pattern of in-migration.

Age Distribution and Household Composition. Between 1970 and 1980 the proportion of California's population between the ages of fifteen and thirty-four years—those most likely to prefer renting—increased from 31 to 37 percent. That proportion is now falling and will probably drop to about 28 percent by the year 2000. At the same time the proportion of mature adults (thirty-five to sixty-four years) will rise from 31 to about 39 percent of total population.[6]

Whereas in 1980 there were 1.2 young adults for every mature adult, by 2000 there will be only 0.7 young adults for every mature adult. Mature adults have higher incomes, steadier jobs, are more likely to have children, and are less prone to move than the younger ones. We should therefore expect a shift from renting to owning as the preferred tenure.

Family Structure and Lifestyle. The emerging generation of home-owners, however, will be less eager than their predecessors to live in detached single-family houses. The proportion of adults who are currently married is dropping, the number of children per household is declining, and the proportion of wives who work outside the home is rising. With smaller households, fewer or no children, and less time spent at home, many homebuyers will look for smaller dwellings, less private outdoor space, and institutional arrangements that reduce their responsibility for maintenance. Continued growth in the popularity of townhouses, multiunit condominiums, and mobile home parks can be expected. As these examples suggest, the traditional distinction between owning and renting will become increasingly blurred.

As that distinction fades, the investment motive will become increasingly salient in tenure choice. Financial institutions are geared to enable people of modest means to make highly leveraged investments only in residential real estate. During the 1970s buying a home was easily the best investment opportunity available to the typical Californian, yielding an average annual return after taxes of nearly 21 percent on a rapidly growing equity.[7]

The speculative boom that made such earnings possible ended in 1980. Since then, a Californian looking for both a place to live and a way to invest his savings can do better financially by renting a home and investing in certificates of deposit or municipal bonds. However, with stable home prices, rising rents, and falling interest rates, the balance of financial advantage is gradually shifting back towards ownership.

It would be fruitless to speculate about the comparative costs of owning and renting in the 1990s. The important point is that as housing preferences shift towards types of dwellings that are readily available either for rent or for sale, comparative costs will be increasingly salient in tenure choice.

Migration and Ethnic Change. The other important change, whose future is less clear, is in the pattern of migration. For many decades half to two-thirds of California's population growth was attributable to net inmigration, mostly from other parts of the United States. Since

1970, however, net inmigration to California of U.S.-born residents of other states has virtually ceased, whereas the number of foreign-born residents of California doubled between 1970 and 1980 and accounted for half of the state's population growth during that decade.[8] Most students of migration believe that these census-based estimates substantially undercount the number of immigrants from abroad, many of whom enter illegally so avoid enumeration or misrepresent their origins.

About half of the immigrants during the 1970s were from Latin countries of the Western Hemisphere, and about one-fourth were Asians. Since 1980 this pattern of Latin and Asian immigration has clearly continued; but it may be modified by whatever laws emerge from Congress's continued deliberations on immigration reform.

Nearly all foreign-born immigrants rent their first dwellings in California, and most enter the economy as casual laborers working for low wages. Both Latins and Asians, however, are anxious to own their homes and move rapidly to ownership status as they find secure jobs and accumulate savings. Even though renting is primarily a transitional arrangement for immigrants, the flow has been so great that if it were halted by new laws the effect would be strongly felt in the low-rent housing market.

The Prospective Supply of Rental Housing

As noted earlier, the supply of rental housing is flexible because dwellings can move from rental to owner-occupancy or the reverse. Such conversions modulate the market imbalances created by bursts of new construction, whether the new units are planned for rent or for sale. It is important to keep in mind that local overbuilding of homes for sale generally adds to the supply of rental housing either directly or indirectly as builders or other property owners search for a way to pay the holding costs while they wait for the sales market to revive.

Investment Motivations. What governs the pace of new rental construction? It is important here to distinguish the motivations of the developer, the mortgage lender, and the long-term equity investor and property manager. Developers are by natural selection optimists about the future. According to Tony Downs, a developer will build anything that a lender will finance, and lenders seem easily charmed by optimistic prospectuses. Anyone who believes in the prudence of bankers these days is indeed a true believer.

The key to the future supply of rental housing is how such investments work out for the long-term equity-owner and property-manager. Hardly anyone thinks that it is fun to be a landlord. The basic motivation for taking an equity position in rental real estate is the expectation of greater long-term investment yields than are otherwise available. It is useful to distinguish four kinds of benefits that professional investors expect.

The first is that, generally speaking, a real estate investment provides a long-term hedge against inflation; almost regardless of the financial performance of a specific property, its nominal market value rises along with prices in general. The second is the prospect of real capital gains arising from local market conditions; many investors believe, correctly or not, that they can anticipate local shifts in population and employment that will drive up the market value of their chosen property faster than general price inflation. The third is the tax shelter provided by depreciation allowances, which especially attracts investors with large current incomes from other sources. The fourth, which interacts with all the others, is that our financial institutions permit a higher degree of leveraging in real estate investments than in most other kinds; the owner of a small equity gets all the capital gains and all the depreciation allowances.

A substantial portion of the rental stock is owned by individuals who can scarcely be called professional investors. They are not characteristically speculators hoping for big capital gains, their investments are not usually highly leveraged, and they gain little from tax shelters. Some became landlords by accident when they changed residences or inherited a house; others built or bought duplexes or small apartment houses as income property to help support retirement. They were encouraged by a quirk in our social security law, which counts earnings from employment as an offset against benefit entitlement but does not count investment earnings. Retirees who buy and personally manage small rental properties treat the implicit return to their labor as investment earnings.

Recent legislation marginally reduces the tax benefits of real estate investment for both high-income professionals and retirees. Some tax reform proposals would further reduce the attractiveness of equity investment in rental property. Increasingly, the investor must look to net operating income rather than appreciation or tax breaks as the reward for investment.

Regulation and Risk. Government regulation of private industry usually balances the limitation of gain by a limitation of risk. This has not been the case with rental housing. Over the past decade state legislation, local ordinances, and court decisions have restricted rents, increased operating costs, complicated management, and raised the risk of civil and criminal liability.

The most conspicuous innovation is public regulation of rents, now widespread in California. Most local ordinances are more decorative than functional; but a few, such as those in Berkeley and Santa Monica, have seriously restricted rents and operating incomes. Nearly all complicate the management of rental property and subject the landlord to the risk of legal actions brought by his tenants.

A second development is fair housing legislation that restricts a landlord's freedom to choose the kinds of tenants he prefers. Under current interpretations of state law and local ordinances, an applicant may not be rejected because of his race, religion, sex, marital status, sexual preference, age, source of income, or household composition. Irrational prejudices aside, landlords have learned that some classes of tenants are more likely than others to damage property, disturb their neighbors, and skip rent payments. They also know that tenants who share cultural assumptions get along better with each other than those whose lifestyles differ. In the interests of fairness to individuals who may not fit the stereotype, our laws now forbid landlords to apply this class knowledge to the management of their property. The inevitable consequences are higher operating costs, more rent loss, and more intertenant conflict.

The third development is a broadening of landlords' civil liability for injuries sustained on their premises by tenants and their visitors. Recent court decisions have held landlords liable for hazards of which they were necessarily ignorant and for hazards created by the tenants themselves. The growing popularity of tort actions and the readiness of juries to vote large damage awards is not confined to renter-landlord relationships but there as elsewhere is raising the cost of liability insurance.

Landlords can learn to live with these developments, but each adds risk and unpleasantness to rental property ownership and management and raises direct operating costs or lowers revenue. Collectively, they discourage investment in rental property, especially by small-holders who lack the sophistication to outwit the intent of the law while adhering to the letter. On the whole, a decline in the proportion of rental dwellings owned by casual investors or held as income properties by elderly people can be expected.

Summary Forecast

Over the next fifteen years there should be slower growth in California's renter population than in recent experience. Unless Congress acts on the Simpson-Mazzoli bill,[9] a growing proportion of renters will be recent immigrants. There will be an expanding market for dwellings that offer some of the benefits of ownership but entail less maintenance responsibility. In addition, tenure choice by prosperous households will respond more readily to shifts in the comparative costs of owning and renting.

On the supply side, local booms in rental housing construction will occur whenever lending institutions have a surplus of loanable funds. Professional investors will look increasingly to net operating income rather than prospective capital appreciation or tax benefits as the litmus of profitability. Market rents will rise at about the same rate as the consumer price index. Rent controls will spread and become increasingly complex. Mom-and-pop landlords will gradually exit from the market.

These expectations combine to form two images of successful rental property. One is the cracker-box apartment building catering to recent immigrants whose main requirement is low rent; it will be professionally managed to minimize maintenance expense and maximize cash flow. The other is the upscale condominium, a mixture of owner-occupied and investor-owned dwellings, the latter occupied by prosperous renters. Missing from this picture is the spacious six-unit middle-class apartment building and the modest frame house managed as a rental property by its former owner-occupants or their heirs.

Notes

1. U.S. Bureau of the Census, *1980 Census of Housing, General Housing Characteristics, California.* HC80-1-A6, Calif. (U.S. Government Printing Office, 1982).

2. Ira S. Lowry, C. E. Hillestad, and S. Sarma, *California's Housing: Adequacy, Availability, and Affordability.* R-3066-CSA Santa Monica, Calif.: The Rand Corporation, October 1983), pp. 79–98.

3. Ibid., Table 4.4.

4. Ibid., Table 4.8.

5. Ibid., Table 4.11.

6. Kevin F. McCarthy and R. B. Valdez, "California's Demographic Future," Tables 3.6 to 3.8; In J. J. Kirlin and D. R. Winkler, eds., *California Policy Choices*, Vol. 2 (Los Angeles: University of Southern California, School of Public Administration, 1985).

7. Ira S. Lowry, *Creative Financing in California: The Morning After.* R-3081-RC (Santa Monica, Calif.: The Rand Corporation, December 1983), Sec. II.

8. McCarthy and Valdez, op. cit., pp. 44–46. See also Joseph DiMento, LeRoy Graymer, and Frank Schnidman, *The Urban Caldron* (Boston, Mass.: Oelgeschlager, Gunn & Hain, 1986).

9. The Immigration Reform and Control Act, Public Law gg-603, was signed by the President on November 6, 1986.

4

Is the California Rental Housing Market Moving Toward a Balance?

Fred E. Case*

Is There a Boomlet in California Rental Housing?

The surge in California home building that began in 1983 promises to carry through to the end of the decade with forecasts of the addition of over 200,000 new housing units annually for 1985, 1986, and 1987, according to the latest UCLA-Graduate School of Management forecast. The expectation is that multifamily (rental) units will represent between 45 and 51 percent of all units built (see Figure 4.1). This growth is expected to continue through 1990 because it will be supported by lower mortgage interest rates, slower increases in housing prices, and continued improvements in employment and personal income. Realization of these expectations could mean that California housing construction and sales markets would be at historically high levels through the end of the decade.

The important question raised by these trends is whether the housing problem peculiar to California markets (i.e., unaffordable housing prices and unavailable moderate-priced rentals) is moving towards solution. Will the anticipated increases in new housing permit the average California family once again to find rental or owner housing within its financial capabilities? Is there a sufficient supply of housing moving into the markets to cause lower rents and prices? Is there a sufficient boomlet in multifamily housing to keep a ceiling on or even reduce rents and improve rental housing availability?

*Real Estate Research Program, Graduate School of Management, U. of California, Los Angeles, Calif.

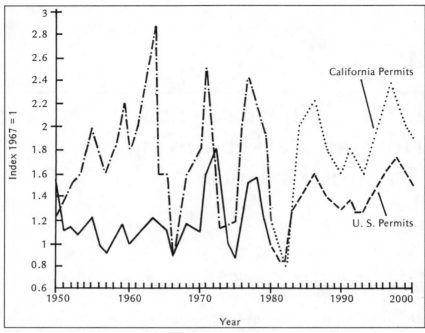

Figure 4.1. *New housing changes, 1950–2000 (United States and California).*

Unfortunately the data do not provide definitive answers nor comfortable conclusions. Instead they permit a spectrum of answers that are only remotely compatible with each other.

The United States and California

The most complete evidence on multifamily markets is found in Bureau of the Census figures on new apartment and condominium construction; and, since California represents such a significant segment of the total U.S. housing construction, some inferences can be drawn about the California rental housing market.

Since 1980 the number of new, unfurnished apartments in buildings with five or more units constructed in the United States has increased from 194,100 in 1980 to 313,900 in 1984 (see Table 4.1). In 1983 and 1984 the number of new units added was more than 60 percent higher than the preceding year. The present rate for the first quarter of 1985 suggests a much slower addition of new units and suggests a 1985 total about 10 percent higher than the 1984 high.

Table 4.1
New Apartment and Condominium Construction in the United States and Western United States, 1980–1985

Unit Type, Characteristics	Multifamily Units Completed, 1980–1984					First Quarter	
	1980	1981	1982	1983	1984	1984	1985
United States							
Apartments unfurnished[a]	194,100	135,500	116,000	191,000	313,900	68,900	75,000
Change from previous year (percent)		−30	−14	65	64		
Percent absorbed in three months	75	80	72	69	70		64
Median rent	$308	$347	$385	$387	$394		$411
Change from previous year (percent)		13	11	1	2		
Cooperative/condominium	125,200	112,500	109,200	112,600	142,900	23,600	32,300
Change from previous year (percent)		−10	−3	3	27		
As percent of total	65	83	94	59	46		
Furnished	9,900	6,100	5,400	4,800	9,900	1,700	1,200
Change from previous year (percent)		−38	−11	−11	106		
As percent of total	5	5	5	3	3		
Western United States							
Apartments unfurnished	44,900	25,100	23,800	32,000	74,600		
Change from previous year (percent)		−44	−5	34	133		
Percent of U.S. total	23	19	21	17	24		
Percent absorbed in three months	74	75	72	70	70		
Percent relative to United States	99	94	100	101	100		
Median rent	$342	$362	$400	$426	$432		
Change from previous year (percent)		6	10	7	1		
Percent relative to United States	111	104	104	110	110		
Cooperative/condominium	35,400	31,800	25,400	22,800	29,200		
Percent of U.S. total	28	28	23	20	20		
Total multiples, United States	329,200	254,100	230,600	308,400	466,700		
Change from previous year (percent)		−23	−9	34	51		

Source: Department of Commerce, Bureau of the Census, *Current Housing Reports, Characteristics of Apartments Completed.* H-131-80A.

[a] Privately financed, nonsubsidized, unfurnished apartments in buildings with five units or more.

The market seems to be demanding these units since at least 70 percent of the 1984 units were absorbed into the market within the first three months that they were for rent; the figure was 64 percent for the first quarter of 1985.

Some possibility of market saturation, or at least a better balance between supply and demand, is suggested by the fact that median rent in 1981 and 1982 increased at rates of 11 and 13 percent, compared to rates of 1 to 4 percent for 1983, 1984, and 1985.

The mix of new multiunit construction has been changing with the introduction of cooperative and condominium construction, which in 1982 equalled more than 90 percent of all multiunits constructed. Since then the rate has dropped to below 50 percent. Available evidence indicates that perhaps as much as 40 percent of these condominium units will be rented. (Furnished apartment units represent an insignificant percent of all new multiunits.)

Since the 1980 Census of Housing indicated that approximately 30 percent of all single-family homes were being rented, the combined effects of more single-family homes, the rate of rentals among cooperative and condominium units, and the actual number of new rental units being added suggest that a modest rental housing boomlet does exist in the United States. Since California dominates the housing market, similar trends should be found there. Unfortunately, comparable statistics do not exist for California, but they do exist for the western states, of which California is the dominant proportion.

The Western United States

The construction of unfurnished apartment units in the western United States is even stronger than for the nation generally; however, the construction pattern has been irregular so that total units have varied from a 1984 high of 24 percent to a 1983 low of 17 percent of all apartment units constructed in the United States. The median rent, which has been much higher than the U.S. median rent, has increased each year but at rates varying between 6 and 10 percent, increasing from 1983 to 1984 by only 1 percent.

California and Southern California

Data about California and southern California rental housing construction can be developed only with many assumptions since new construction information on multiunits is lacking in important details.

Since 1950 multiunits have ranged from a 1955 low of 15 percent to a 1970 high of 64 percent of all new housing units constructed in California. Since 1980 they have ranged between 40 and 59 percent of all new units and seem likely in 1985 to equal less than 50 percent of all new housing units (see Table 4.2).

Table 4.2
Multifamily Units as Percent of Total New Construction in California and Southern California, 1950–1985

Year	Cali-fornia	Seven Counties	Los Angeles	Orange	River-side	San Bernardo	San Diego	Santa Barbara	Ventura
1950	33	34	35	32	20	30	30	25	22
1951	32	33	34	31	18	27	26	20	19
1952	27	28	28	26	17	19	25	18	13
1953	21	24	26	20	15	16	23	11	11
1954	18	19	21	18	10	11	21	10	10
1955	15	18	19	16	10	18	17	12	13
1956	22	26	34	11	15	11	18	20	12
1957	35	38	52	23	18	10	30	22	14
1958	38	43	59	33	19	12	31	28	15
1959	34	37	52	38	13	15	23	29	13
1960	39	41	58	33	19	15	20	21	12
1961	44	46	61	38	23	16	30	25	13
1962	51	54	69	45	29	34	37	37	23
1963	59	62	75	52	35	39	45	49	22
1964	58	62	74	54	43	45	56	59	21
1965	46	53	66	32	45	27	47	70	29
1966	34	38	50	29	18	20	42	40	20
1967	39	43	56	29	26	8	49	60	21
1968	46	60	58	44	31	19	56	58	15
1969	57	69	70	61	35	17	57	64	30
1970	64	60	82	78	49	36	57	68	53
1971	56	62	75	52	52	40	54	54	60
1972	56	57	80	50	47	40	62	67	46
1973	53	50	78	45	43	29	48	70	54
1974	41	36	71	43	20	16	52	53	33
1975	31	40	50	35	55	9	40	27	26
1976	37	40	51	43	46	7	46	38	30
1977	35	49	55	43	20	7	50	32	21
1978	42	49	67	51	27	27	54	44	35
1979	40	50	67	49	32	28	49	31	23
1980	40	50	71	36	29	26	51	34	31
1981	43	53	71	54	27	24	57	25	29
1982	41	48	69	46	17	29	50	42	43
1983	57	46	65	42	18	33	48	30	35
1984	59	55	67	44	37	47	64	52	49
1985	46	55	70	44	35	48	62	50	34

Source: Southern California Residential Research Council, California Department of Finance, UCLA-Graduate School of Management Forecasting Project.

Multiunits in the seven southern California counties tend to be a larger percent of all new units than is true in the rest of the state. Among the seven counties in 1985, multiunits range from a low of 30 percent of all new units in Ventura County to 70 percent of all new units in Los Angeles County (see Figure 4.2).

The best general reflection of rent levels is found in the Cost of Housing Index for Los Angeles, which since 1980 has risen from 210 to 309 in the first quarter of 1985—increases that are substantially higher than for the United States. Such increases undoubtedly help explain the preponderance of multiunit construction in Los Angeles County as compared to the other southern counties.

Do these rental housing construction trends indicate a boomlet? The answer is yes when they are compared to more recent historical trends. If, however, approximately one-half of the multiunit construc-

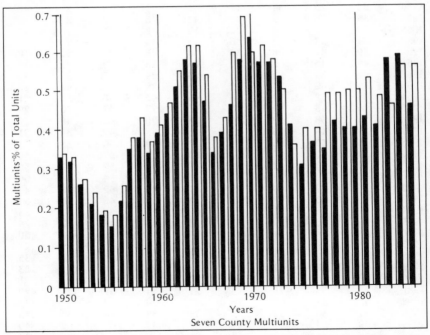

Figure 4.2. *Multiunits, percent of permits for seven counties (1950–1985).*

tion is cooperative and condominium construction (as is true nationally), then only 60 to 70 percent of the multifamily units will be rental units. Even though some proportion of the new single-family home construction may be rented, the high cost of new residential construction seems to indicate that there will be little relief in the upward surge of rents.

A reasonable conclusion from all of this evidence suggests that what appears to be a boomlet in multiunit construction may not be very significant because it may be only a part of a long-term catch-up with the continuing demand pressures for lower-cost rental housing. It is still open to debate whether or not market distortions caused by rent and growth controls have influenced these trends and the extent of such distortions. The evidence that has been reviewed is certainly inconclusive about long-term rental market outcomes.

In What Areas May Boomlets Exist and Why?

An unfortunate habit of many housing forecasters is to speak of United States, California, or southern California housing markets, implying that there is a uniformity of market activity in these areas. California and southern California are really a complex of local markets, with each having special characteristics that make it unique in some aspect. Within these local markets, however, inferences about rental markets can be drawn only from overall housing data.

Differences in housing market characteristics in California are a function of changes in population, income, geography, and local governmental land use and rent controls. Increasing population and rising personal income have been the basic forces supporting market trends—particularly, changes in the numbers and types of new housing units constructed. Population changes, compared to construction and personal income changes, have been particularly erratic, but changes in these three factors have tended to move at similar rates (see Figure 4.3). A reflection of changes in basic housing market trends in local (county) housing markets can be found in overall California housing data.

Since 1950 California population changes have varied from year to year, increasing from 1950 to 1965 and moving slowly downward since 1965, and they will probably continue downward until 2000. During this same period new housing permits have increased at a fairly consistent rate, and housing prices have continued to rise relentlessly. Improving personal income, when reinforced by local political conditions that

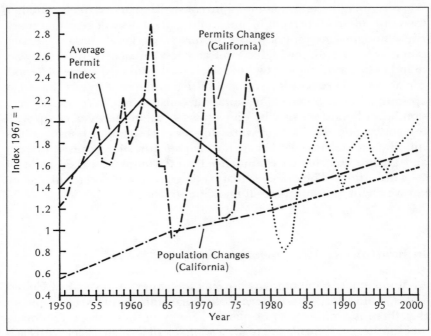

Figure 4.3. *California population/permits indices, 1950–2000 (1967 = 100).*

constrain new construction in desirable living areas, has skewed housing construction in favor of higher-priced owner-occupied housing.

A closer look at local housing markets reflected in county market data, however, reveals some interesting differences. Rates of construction of new homes, the mix between rental and owner housing, rents, and prices differ markedly among various counties.

The best reflection of the mix of statewide housing trends is found in the seven southern California counties that include more than one-half of all new housing construction. There are marked differences both within and among the counties as Table 4.2 indicates. In Los Angeles county, for example, average housing prices ranged from a high of $1,030,000 to a low of $75,000. The average county home prices among the seven counties ranged from a high average of $161,000 in Los Angeles county to a low average of $97,828 in the Riverside-San Bernardino counties.

Presumably, rental prices also would show the same differences within and among counties. Given the relationships existing between owned and rented housing, some tentative conclusions can be drawn about where the most active rental markets exist.

The strongest public and political constraints on housing are generally found in the coastal counties. These are also the most heavily urbanized and contain families with the highest median incomes. The result is that the population growth produces pressures for more intensive land uses; and, given the scarcity of inexpensive buildable residential land, these pressures can be met only with multifamily housing. Given the higher personal incomes in these areas, however, multifamily construction is more likely to be condominium/cooperative or higher-price rental housing. Subsidies would seem to be the only answer to lower-priced housing or rentals in these areas. This is what seems to be happening in Marin, San Francisco, San Jose, Monterey, Santa Barbara, Los Angeles, Orange, Riverside, and San Diego counties.

In southern California counties, for example, the percentage of housing permits in multifamily units in 1985 was expected to equal 70 percent in Los Angeles, 62 percent in San Diego, and 50 percent in Santa Barbara. And these are the counties with the highest home prices.

Given the attraction of coastal living and the higher prices and more restricted housing activities in the counties mentioned, the second tier of adjacent counties with somewhat lower percentages of multifamily housing are Ventura (34 percent) and Riverside (35 percent). However, boomlets in rental housing are most likely to occur in these counties primarily because of lower land and construction prices and lower personal incomes. These are the locations to which more and more employers are or will be moving to reduce their labor costs and attract employees seeking less crowded living and lower home ownership or rental costs.

The second most likely rental boomlet markets will be found in the inland counties, such as San Bernardino or Sacramento counties and the counties in the San Joaquin valley. The attraction the inland counties have for increased population and new housing is reflected best in San Bernardino county, the largest county in the United States. This county is also reasonably close to major coastal employment. In San Bernardino county multifamily units equaled 48 percent of all housing units in permits in 1985. This percentage reflects, to some extent, the historical percentages in California housing markets before current inflationary and restrictive growth pressures existed. San Bernardino is most likely to have a balance between owning or renting so that prices and supply should provide affordable units for approximately 50 to 60 percent of the families seeking ownership as well as affordable rental housing of choice for the remainder of the families.

Will the Boomlets Be Sustained?

At this point it should be clear that there is no such thing as a California rental housing boomlet, but there are boomlets in certain county or local markets.

Even though California housing markets should be considered as a series of local markets with differing characteristics, they all have a common dependence upon general economic conditions. They are also strongly influenced by unexpected external forces, particularly national forces. For example, until monetary and fiscal policies support long-term lower mortgage interest rates, housing markets are not likely to show continued buoyancy. Fortunately, California is somewhat insulated from many kinds of national economic traumas, and many counties are somewhat insulated from state economic traumas. For these reasons, improving housing markets (following trends already occurring in individual counties) are expected to continue through 1990. Given the presidential elections in 1988, no significant change in housing market trends resulting from changes in national economic and housing policies is expected. No matter what party may be in power at the time, housing market trends inevitably sag in the year or two following the election year. No party, however, is urging the introduction of massive programs favoring housing similar to those that supported the improving markets of the 1950s and early 1960s. Housing will continue to be the marginal element in economic planning, with its levels and strength dependent upon major economic policies.

In spite of the very apparent difficulties of forecasting housing market trends, something can be learned from reviewing housing market trends of the last 130 years. To change a familiar phrase, by learning history we may be able to repeat it.

An interesting historical perspective can be obtained by looking at real estate sales activity in Los Angeles County since 1850. This provides insights into the struggles between demand and supply to reach some kind of equilibrium, even though the patterns are most erratic.

The first lesson from history is that market turns cannot be forecasted, except by accident. Every turn in housing markets has been produced by forces outside of the market. In recent years the monetary crunch of 1966, the inflation of the late 1970s, and deflation have all changed the direction of housing market sales activities.

Since such exogenous events cannot be anticipated, long-run market trends exclusive of them can be extrapolated. A duplication of long-term market patterns suggests reasonably strong housing markets through

2000. The current upward market movement seems destined to carry through 1988, to decline through 1994, and to revive until 2000.

Will rental markets share in these trends? Again history suggests that greater coastal population densities accompanied by improving personal income will inevitably force denser housing in those areas, particularly since people do seem to prefer coastal living. However, high incomes can also produce a strong demand for rental housing since historically a significant percentage of all families do not want home ownership.

The ripple effects of coastal housing markets will be felt in the most adjacent counties, sparking periodic rental housing boomlets. The most dynamic housing boomlets will occur in the inland counties, which will benefit from the spillovers from the coastal counties as employers seek less costly locations and families seek affordable rental and owner housing.

5

The California Rental
Housing Market:
A Commentary

In this chapter housing experts describe the nature of the rental housing problem, available information for analysis of public policy on rental housing, and the human impact of the gap in housing supply.

* * *

BEN BARTOLOTTO: In terms of the current and long-term outlooks for housing production, specifically in rental housing production, I expect to see a higher level than the UCLA Forecast would indicate. As far as the long-term outlook, I am much more pessimistic.

On the statewide housing production levels, the August 1985 figures show about 148,000 multifamily housing units for the seasonably adjusted, annualized rate. That's four times the 1982 level of multifamily housing production, but 1982 was a very deep recession for housing, especially in this state. We have to view 1982 realizing that interest rates peaked at around 15 to 16 percent and the prime rate went on to 20 percent plus. The outlook for housing in those years was not very good. It was also the lowest yearly production level in the state since the end of World War II.

Looking back a little farther, these current August figures are comparable with the 1972 level for the same month—151,000 units was the annual rate for that month in 1972—although they are lower than what I think is the all-time high shown in 1963 of nearly 200,000 units annualized. For the state as a whole, if we look at a six-year period—and forget vacancy rates that you have to add to household growth—rental housing production has actually lagged behind renter household growth with the exception of the last two years, when rental housing production has exceeded the renter household growth. When we look at specific counties, we find quite a bit of difference. The only county that stands out as being substantially above what the renter household growth might indicate is Los Angeles, where in the last two years we estimate production of rental housing at 21,000 units plus, compared with increases in renter households above 1984 of about 13,700. But we also have to keep in mind that that was also a very tight market. In 1980 the census showed a rental vacancy rate of only 3.9 percent in Los Angeles County compared with a 5.1 percent rental vacancy rate for the state as a whole. So while we are probably facing a short-term oversupply condition in Los Angeles, there is enough potential household growth and a low enough vacancy rate to absorb that over a short period of time.

The increase in multifamily housing in the state this year to a large extent has been due to two counties: Los Angeles and Sacramento. If we add the numbers from last year and this year, we could also include San Diego County as showing a very substantial rate of increase. With the exception of Los Angeles, however, both San Diego and Sacramento have really failed to keep pace in the first six years of the decade with their average household growth. San Diego is slightly ahead, but again it had vacancy rates so it is probably really behind. Sacramento is also running slightly behind. With the exception of the last two years, when we have had a surge of activity in rental housing production, this trend is probably aided by at least two factors. One is the rental mortgage revenue bond programs, which have become much more widespread, and the other is the uncertainty created by tax reform which probably has caused some projects to be advanced that might not have moved otherwise. People are anxious because they do not know what tax reform is going to bring, although everyone expects it is going to be somewhat negative for rental housing in the future.

As far as the longer term outlook, maybe on the order of 25 percent of all rental units produced in the first six years of the decade had some form of subsidy, most significantly the revenue bond program. The outlook for that kind of subsidy in the future is not very optimistic. With or without tax reform the mortgage revenue bond program is facing a very stiff fight just to remain in existence, and I predict that it will no longer be available as a support for the rental housing picture. When you take that out of the last six years, then the picture is not as rosy as these numbers might indicate; we would have fallen well behind these estimates of renter household growth.

I differ a little with Ira Lowry's consumption model approach to the issue of whether or not we have enough housing in general—and specifically rental housing. Lowry points out that per household consumption of rental housing increased from 1970 to 1980 by 6 percent per household. Consumption is measured by a combination of factors. It takes into consideration fiscal characteristics of the dwelling unit as well as operational features—for example, the number of rooms, kinds of domestic equipment, and operating input such as fuel and utility services. When you look at this analysis by category of household, you do not find the increase is across the board. In the sixty-five-year-old and older group per household consumption dropped 10 percent, and in the very-low- and low-income groups, housing consumption dropped per person. I suspect that in those areas where you did find consumption increasing, a lot of that had to do with a very significant social change where household size declined—for example, higher divorce rates, the fact that the largest age group is twenty to thirty years old, and the tendency toward smaller households. I tend to like to look in terms of how many housing units are needed. What are those housing units, and where is the growth occurring? If you look at where the strong growth areas are compared with how much housing is actually being produced in terms of units, prices, and rents, I do not think that the findings would be as rosy as the study suggests.

I also expect to see more demand or need for rental housing because of the changing characteristics of the population. Most of our immigration is and will be Latin; and, according to the 1980 census, 60 percent of that group rented in 1980, and probably at least that percentage of new immigrants will be renters in the future. Secondly, the outlook for ownership housing was not very strong in the first part of the 1980s; in spite of the recovery, we are still well below the level we expected given the drop in interest rates. I think the difficulty of getting into ownership housing is going to remain with us as long as mortgage interest rates are higher than they should be relative to inflation.

LeRoy Graymer: We always have to take a look at these statistics in terms of how we are doing on the average, and then we must move on to the question: How does that data affect the various populations within our population? Taking a bit more of a microscopic view into what the people at the Bay Area Council have looked at might help us understand some of the micromarkets.

Bradley Inman: There are three points I want to cover. The first is that some of our information lacks peripheral vision. The second point is that something that we in the public policy field fail to watch is the behavior of the building community. And third, where will our renters live?

First, we lack sufficient data. Looking at the period from 1980 to 1985, we do not have a good set of data to make informed decisions on public policy as it relates to rental housing. Groups like ours are forced to do as much research as we can on local markets, but in terms of statewide policy, we are really in trouble. We have Security Pacific Bank information on new starts, counted by county, month to month, quarter to quarter, year by year; but we have no idea what proportion of those multifamily permits are actually rental housing. From the Federal Home Loan Bank of San Francisco, we know that the vacancy rate in the nine-county Bay Area is 1.2 percent for multifamily housing, but we have no idea if that includes the bankrupt condo projects on the shore in San Francisco. We do know the rental component of the CPI, but we have no idea what the average rent is for a two-bedroom apartment in California. Finally, we have a lot of capital chasing rental housing in the Bay Area, which is contributing to a major rental housing construction boom. In light of having all this capital, we see some decisions that are not based on good market research. An analogy dates from a couple years ago. When a large manufacturer in San Francisco went to build a high-rise, the EIR said the traffic service level from the high-rise would be at D level. The fact is that there were six other concurrent proposals for the area, and the net effect would be a minus service level. A similar phenomenon is true of market research: too often market research only looks at specific projects and not the net aggregate effect.

A few comments specifically on the papers: The point that the whole price market is changing is important. We have seen a stabilization of home prices, incomes are going up (at least in the Bay Area), and interest rates are coming down. Up-scale yuppies who traditionally could not afford a new home are moving out of the rental market into the for-sale market. That a lot of builders are building to the up-scale yuppie market will result in cross-collateralization—all going off after that market segment that is very affluent. As yuppies move into the first-time home, the demand for rental housing is affected particularly as it relates to the production phenomena.

In terms of rent price hikes, we have information on the advertised rents in the Bay Area from 1980 to 1985. We did an annual survey: from 1980 to 1982, the median-priced two-bedroom apartment went up 6.7 percent; from 1982 to 1983, 9.3 percent; from 1983 to 1984, about 13.3 percent; and from 1984 to 1985, 16.7 percent. The aggregate is 75 percent rent hikes for a two-bedroom apartment. While there may be some rent stabilization in Los Angeles, we see rapid rent hikes in the Bay Area.

There is a production boom, but at least in the Bay Area it follows a complete lack of production. Between 1976 and 1979, we had an annual production rate for twenty cities serving the nine-county Bay Area of 4,500 rental housing units, and from 1979 to 1983, it was down to 1500 units per year; but in 1984 alone we had permits for about 8000 units and proposals for about 19,000. Looking only at 1984 suggests that the boomlet is solving the problem, but it is a hiatus after a ten-year "dry hole."

A second point: too often people in public policy, academia, and local officials ignore the effect on public policy of production decisions by builders, particularly the effect on boom-and-bust cycles. Boom-and-bust cycles are a function of capital and other factors, but they are also a function of behavior by the building community. Houston is a good example. A sheep went down there early, smelled something good, and a herd followed. We see that in the nine-county Bay Area, and certain markets within the region are ignored and others are being overbuilt to a potentially dangerous degree. Our concern is the regional impact of this; if there is some overbuilding and some fallout, the whole regional market itself will be in danger.

My final point concerns the affordability problem. As I mentioned, in the nine-county Bay Area rents have gone up 75 percent; during that period, the CPI went up 33 percent and personal income went up 38 percent. The rapid increase in rents in the early 1980s is pricing a large part of our population out of the market. Over a five-to-ten-year period, it will be hard to recover. We estimate in San Francisco alone that 70 percent of the households cannot afford the median-priced two-bedroom apartment. For the Bay Area as a whole, we estimate that 55 percent could not afford that average two-bedroom apartment.

FRED KAHANE: It is my opinion that there is a total lack of public policy leadership in terms of housing policy at the federal, state, and local government levels. Answering housing problems by turning them over to the private market leaves something lacking.

The income of the average renter is two-thirds that of the average homeowner. Almost three-quarters of the total renters are in low- or moderate-income households as defined by federal standards. So when we talk about rental housing policy, we are talking about policies affecting the low- and moderate-income households. Government's role should be to help those that can least help themselves; in the housing field we are generally talking about renters.

In southern California's rental sector, there has been a fairly rapid increase in construction. But the supposed boomlet is really nothing more than a response to market forces. The supply of rental housing goes up and down in direct response to total supply. We are just building more rental units in direct relationship to total production, which varies over the years.

The yearly regional totals for multifamily housing production show that 1970 was the zenith year when almost 70 percent of our construction was in multifamily units. (At that time it was almost all rentals; there were no condominiums being built.) At the low point, which was 1975, multiunit construction dropped almost half, to 35 percent of all new construction. Since then it has been creeping upward. If you remember, 1975 was the credit-crunch year, the year of overbuilding, and a few years after the earthquake when our population was leaving in droves. Many market forces contributed to this, and public policy has had very little to do with the amount of rental housing construction—it is more of an afterthought.

What's causing the boomlet now? Rents have been escalating about 9 to 10 percent in southern California, and the rent increases have gone up faster than cost increases in construction, in interest and financing costs generally, as well as in operational and maintenance costs. There have also been improvements in the attractiveness of investing in rental property as compared to alternative real estate investments, particularly office buildings or other forms of investment. Such factors include stable or diminishing interest costs, particularly through the use of mortgage revenue bonds; the availability of equity and investment capital; the subsidence of rent control regulations and various state legislative attempts to curb rent control further; the liberalization of depreciation benefits in the early 1980s in the different tax acts; and the high cost of single-family home ownership. Then there are some localized factors, such as the boom in recreational area construction and the selling of investment-opportunity condominiums, many of which are later rented. Measured by per capita construction of multifamily units in southern California, nine out of the top ten building areas are in Riverside and San Bernardino County. Almost all of them are in the desert or recreational communities; but the exception is Irvine, which has a specific public policy that tends—through a corporation, not a local government—to build apartments. Other factors are: the conduciveness of some localities to support urban growth, particularly in desert areas; the changing attitude in growth areas and in innercity areas toward higher density housing; the large influx of immigrants into the region— who rent at an 83 percent rate compared with current residents who rent at 42 percent; the tendency of immigrants to have lower incomes than current residents, therefore having a greater propensity to become renters; the tendency to allow for much higher density in innercity neighborhoods, where political organization tends to be less vocal; the increasing use of recycled land and in-fill properties, which by their location have very high land-cost structures that necessitate higher-density multiunit construction. There has also been a decrease in local growth moratoriums.

The apartment market in general is a leftover market from the single-family ownership market, and it will continue to be so. Public policy generally tends to ignore it.

AUDIENCE QUESTION: Mr. Lowry made a statement that in the future people who buy apartment houses will buy them on their own merits rather than looking for tax ramifications or a hedge from inflation. As a property owner who accumulated a lot of property because of not being smart and because of inflation and tax factors, I want to ask how do you buy a piece of property and let it stand on its two feet if it is leveraged at all?

IRA LOWRY: I am suggesting two things: one, that the prospects for federal tax legislation seem to be that the value of depreciation allowances to investors will diminish in the future; and two, I find it very hard to imagine anything like the appreciation of real estate values that occurred in California during the 1970s occurring again in the next five or ten years. If those two assumptions are true and if investors perceive them to be true, they have to give more weight to operating income than they have in the past. It has not been rare in the past for someone to buy an apartment house with the expectation of a negative cash flow for some time into the future. I do not think that kind of a purchase will look very attractive in the future.

AUDIENCE QUESTION: What percentage of people do you think is moving from the renter status into home-ownership status? Is it strictly by income or are there different demographic characteristics for the group that moves into home ownership?

IRA LOWRY: I estimate that something close to 90 percent of all heads of households in California at some point in their lives will be homeowners. I know that to be true in other markets where I have been able to gather specific data on that subject. That kind of longitudinal data does not exist for California, but it looks to me that that is not far off. This is something that we generally do not realize. At the present time, something like 45 percent of our population rents; there will always be many more renters than there are people who have always been renters.

AUDIENCE QUESTION: Why is home ownership such a great value, and why does everybody take for granted that home ownership is the only way to go?

IRA LOWRY: I do not take that assumption for granted. It is a recurrent theme in American life that home purchase is the best way for people of moderate means to leverage their investments, and that is true. But it is not always a very rewarding investment. So far as the choice of tenure on other grounds, there are arguments both ways. Generally speaking, people whose future is uncertain and who do not like to keep house prefer renting.

FRED CASE: We focus too much on home ownership. What we really need is a good investment analysis of renting versus owning. If homeowners were honest about their costs and returns, more people would prefer renting.

AUDIENCE COMMENT: But that is not the reason most homeowners are homeowners. I do not think everyone sits down and does a cost/benefit analysis. What they want to have is stability in their housing costs, and they also want the privilege of being able to hammer a nail into the wall.

FRED CASE: Perhaps, but I think that is another myth that we ought to look at. There are a lot of people who never want to own a home. It is too much work and too much cost, and the investment return is too uncertain. If I am a good investment analyst, I probably can do better with my excess income as a renter than I could by owning a home.

AUDIENCE QUESTION: To what do you attribute a 75 percent rent increase in San Francisco in five years, which is much bigger than in Los Angeles, which has the same amount of rent control?

BRADLEY INMAN: Vacancies are a factor. In San Francisco we have 275,000 multifamily units, and the Federal Home Loan Bank estimates that the multifamily-unit vacancy rate is one-half of 1 percent. Some experts say that during the 1970s rents lagged behind inflation so that there was room for those rent hikes. Another factor (shown in a study we did about two years ago) is the percentage of income spent on rent by the average renter in the Bay Area; it was lower than the national average, so there was room for some rent increase. That is not to say, however, that the increase has not priced a lot of people out of the market.

In terms of rent control, the boom is concentrated in certain markets. They are building in moderate rent control cities, but they are not building in some of the tighter rent control markets. I do not think you can conclusively say that they are not building in San Francisco because of its type of rent control, but that has been a factor for investors and developers. We have very high land costs, so it is difficult to build rental housing in San Francisco anyway, but rent control also has been a factor. They are not building significantly in Berkeley, if at all.

IRA LOWRY: The Bureau of Labor Statistics rent index for the San Francisco Bay region doesn't show anything like the rate of increase that Mr. Inman gave us. And the FHLB's vacancy rates, whatever virtues they may have, are not in the least comparable to the Bureau of Census data. The 0.5 percent vacancy, if it is interpreted in the same way as one would interpret the Bureau of Census vacancy rate, is absolutely impossible. It is an event that could not happen.

BRADLEY INMAN: The rental component of the CPI during the period 1980 to 1985 in the San Francisco Bay area went up 55 percent. There is a difference. The figure we used was based on advertised—which are not contract—rents. On that basis, the median two-bedroom apartment, we estimated, went up 75 percent. But 55 percent for the rental component of the CPI is still significantly higher than the increase in personal income and the increase in the overall CPI rate for the Bay Area.

AUDIENCE QUESTION: Mr. Kahane mentioned that public policy has to address the needs of lower- or moderate-income families. In an environment of rent control, how much of that policy should government really be required to make? Why shouldn't I insist that prices be lower in Beverly Hills so I can live there when all I can afford to do is live in Hollywood?

FRED KAHANE: I think we first need to get some things in order. The drop-off in apartment construction happened after 1975, way before rent controls were instituted in various cities in southern California. Rent controls were instituted to preserve low- and moderate-income housing, not to build it. No rent control advocate maintains that rent control boosts production. We have abandoned the production levels we need to sustain the kind of market that will produce rents people can afford. Production is the answer. Rent control is not the answer. It is a response to people saying "we can't take this any more." It is also very interesting that rent levels have gone up much higher and much faster since 1980, and there has been a drop-off in rent control legislation at the local government level versus the 1975–1980 period. It is not a question of fairness or equity; rent control was there to stop an erosion of the low- and moderate-income housing stock because we are not producing it.

AUDIENCE QUESTION: There have been numerous studies over the years on the also-growing issue of growth control and other land-use restrictions and how they affect rental markets, multiunits, and home ownership itself. Many economists seem to believe that there are indeed disincentives to future construction created by the proliferation of land-use controls in California.

FRED CASE: There are regions in which there is a complexity of rent controls, environmental controls, growth controls, Proposition 13 controls, and so forth, that produces what I call the red counties. They are all coastal counties, and they reflect very clearly, in prices and in rents, the impact of these combinations of controls without a general policy or a well-stated goal.

FRED KAHANE: The real issue is not the amount of explicit growth control moratoria that have been passed by local governments. They are really down from what they were in the late 1970s as a result of a lot of environmental concerns. The real issue is neighborhood opposition that comes up at every city council, regardless of where you go, when you want to build a multifamily or higher-density project. That permeates the society in southern California. Even if you did not build any housing in all the cities that have growth control moratoria, we would still probably be able to build enough housing in southern California to meet the need. What we cannot seem to get around are public attitudes towards rental and high-density housing.

BEN BARTOLOTTO: Part of the increase in production in Los Angeles county is attributed to the court-ordered conformity between local zoning and the general plan, which would result in a general downzoning of the area. A lot of projects probably moved ahead, in spite of market conditions, to get in under the wire on that likely change in zoning.

LEROY GRAYMER: We have seen a real estate market in which rents have risen very rapidly over the past four to five years. Also, since 1982 there has been a downward trajectory in the interest rate, and people are looking at prospective changes in federal tax policies. This suggests that people may rush to get some building in under the current tax law. Yet it seems that the rate of building of new units does not seem to be as brisk as you would expect. Have I misunderstood?

BEN BARTOLOTTO: One reason it is not as brisk as you might expect is the other factor in the equation: interest rates are still very high compared to historical rates, and that affects the costs of producing these units and of financing them in the long term. That is another factor that did not exist in the climate of the 1970s, at least the early 1970s when rates were much more moderate.

FRED CASE: We do not have good economics in the marketplace. If I'm going to build a house, I am going to sell on the basis of the square-foot price. If I am going to build a rental product and sell it in the marketplace, is it priced by the square foot? By no means. We can get the same price for any number of square feet. We have not made an economically rational market. If the rental market were rational, the price for rental housing would be the price per square foot times the level of usage minus the cost assumed by the tenant.

BRADLEY INMAN: Production is brisk in the Bay Area, and it is good public policy to continue production to avoid the glitches and to promote stabilization in rent increases. But that does not mean that you single-handedly rely on that option; there are other things that have to be done. But to promote an increase in production through whatever mechanisms we can use is good public policy.

AUDIENCE QUESTION: There has been no definition of the housing crisis. Give me a definition of a rental housing situation that is not a crisis. What is it that you view as the objective? Give me just two criteria: give me the essence of crowding, give me the essence of the rent-to-income ratio. What is a rental noncrisis?

IRA LOWRY: I am not sure what the rental housing problem is. It is very difficult, therefore, to provide solutions for it. It would be very helpful if it were clear what the problem is and if the assertions to that effect were supported by some sort of evidence.

FRED CASE: I was talking about boomlets; if the historic increase that we have now is good, that is a boomlet. On the other hand, if we ask, "Are enough people getting cheap housing?," the answer is no. I did not say anything about a crisis.

BEN BARTOLOTTO: I would not use the word *crisis*. I am not sure if we have ever had a real crisis except possibly during severe conditions like war or the Depression. I look in terms of production, what levels you would expect to produce under certain conditions, and what you would expect in terms of household growth. I look at the level of subsidy that we have had over the last few years in terms of the mortgage revenue bond programs and realize the likelihood of that disappearing over the next year or so; I see that as a serious problem in terms of production keeping up with household growth.

BRADLEY INMAN: Seventy percent of the households in the city of San Francisco cannot afford median-priced two-bedroom apartments. I know we need to do something about that figure. And I think the other measure [of a crisis] is the effect high housing costs are having on dislocation in what has been a centralized economy in the region and the effect that has on planning, development patterns, public investment for transportation, and so forth. The problem of high housing costs in the rental market and the for-sale market has affected that dislocation.

AUDIENCE COMMENT: We have very good data on dislocation in terms of journey to work, and it has not been all that marked despite folklore to the contrary. What is your definition of *dislocation*?

BRADLEY INMAN: The development of multiple employment centers in the Bay Area is affecting the quality of life in the region. That feeling comes from both the business perspective and others—and it is also affecting the amount and level of public investment in transportation. Our commute sheds are expanding with this dislocation. Maybe they are not expanding here in southern California, but they are in the Bay Area.

FRED KAHANE: I do not remember using the term *crisis*. The market approach says a healthy vacancy rate is 5 percent, give or take a percentage point. We disagree on how you measure that, but it is generally accepted that we are not close to that rate (unless you count unfinished buildings the way the census did). We have a lower vacancy rate than 5 percent. The market approach is also giving the consumer a wide variety of choices in living environments and a wide variety of rents in various communities throughout the region.

Getting down to what is a crisis, consider the fact that 803,000 households in southern California pay more than the federal standard for rent. From Ira Lowry's study we found out that rent-to-income ratios got better: for the elderly 66 to 60 percent. That is a crisis when you are elderly and you have to pay 60 percent of your income for housing. We are talking about social policy; we are not talking about economics anymore. We are not talking about something the market can serve, obviously. We need to take a stance. If we can afford to spend two billion dollars on a B-1 bomber, we can also afford to take care of 75,000 people who live on the streets.

AUDIENCE QUESTION: There are a number of factors for which we do not have information. Shouldn't one of the factors of public policy be factual data? Shouldn't we be looking at some method by which we could get and obtain data on a better basis than the decennial census? Isn't that one of the things we could ask for, and couldn't we try to get some level of the government to provide better factual data on the basis of which policy decisions could be made?

FRED CASE: We are sharing ignorance in large volume. I have tried to get the state legislature to provide some funding or at least to collect certain data. This has very low priority.

AUDIENCE QUESTION: You put condominiums, townhouses, and planned-unit developments into the rental, multiple-housing category. Condominiums and planned-unit developments are actually single-family homes; they are not rental housing.

IRA LOWRY: My response is brief. A condominium that is rented is rental housing.

6

Fair City: A Case Study in Providing Affordable Housing

The Setting and the Challenge

Fair City is a community of 200,000 people located in an area of the state that has recently attracted a great deal of high-technology industry. In recent years the city has experienced a modest growth rate. Most of the housing needs of professional and related service people brought to Fair City have been met. The average cost of a new single-family home is over $100,000.

The situation for nonprofessional workers is quite the contrary. The cost of a home in Fair City is prohibitive for many of the manufacturing and other blue-collar people who work in the city. Indeed, the best data available, which are not precise, indicate that a full 50 percent of these workers must commute from outside the city in order to find affordable housing.

In Fair City the number of rental units that fall within the state's definition of affordable is very small. Rental housing is mainly located in that part of the city that borders on its more heavily industrial core. Multiple-family residential housing is allowed only in this area. It is an R-3 (defined as minimum apartment house—12.9 units per acre).

Fair City's general plan articulates a much different scenario for the city. Indeed the plan notes that "a decent home in a decent environment is the goal of planning and development of Fair City. It is the city's aim to provide both rental and for-purchase options to those people who work within Fair City whose incomes are between 80 and 120 percent of the median income for the State." Fair City has no rent control ordinance.

More Fair is a group of citizens from various community and church groups in and outside of the city. The citizens have joined together to work on the housing problem in the city. More Fair has met on three occasions and articulated its objective: to provide at least 1,200 units of rental housing in the city of Fair City within the next three years. These units will be affordable to all who work in Fair City, no matter what their incomes. The units will be scattered throughout all sections of the city, and densities will be compatible with the densities of other residential areas of the City.

More Fair has raised $100,000 from private contributions. There are no restrictions on the uses to be made of these monies. The council make-up of Fair City is as follows: two members feel that the market has already provided enough affordable housing and that no changes should be made in the planning or zoning of the community for purposes of increasing the amount of housing: "We really have enough problems in Fair City." Both opponents of more rental housing won re-election handily. Two other council persons are new and have not expressed their views on the matter. The fifth council member is an outspoken fair housing advocate who promotes rapid growth while meeting the housing needs of the less affluent. On three different occasions the old council voted against rezoning for apartments concluding that the environmental impact of high density would be negative.

More Fair representatives have met with the city manager of Fair City and have been told that the city has done all it can do. The manager said that "there really are no significant federal or state funds available these days . . . as much as we try, we can't move state and federal government to help." He also reminded the More Fair group that the city had floated a bond issue to generate revenue for low- and moderate-income housing but that the voters had turned it down.

More Fair has had preliminary discussions with a well-known apartment-house-builder. The builder has pencilled out the cost of units under the constraints of Fair City development control law and regulations and has concluded that he could not build units affordably.

Fair City is the home of another active citizen group, recently formed, called Balanced Growth. Its main platform is to limit all growth in the community, but its charter indicates that "we are particularly concerned with high density development. Our surveys have shown that 85 percent of the citizens of Fair City are opposed to additional apartment housing in the city."

What should More Fair do with its seed money? What else should it do to realize its goals? Can it realize its goals?

JOHN DANNER: What should More Fair do with its seed money? What else should it do to realize its goals? Can it realize its goals? From an attorney's point of view, it seems that the easier client to represent in this case study would be Balanced Growth, not More Fair, because More Fair has a very difficult climb ahead if it is to accomplish its goal of 1,200 units in the next three years.

It is clear that these folks are in for a long fight. This is a conflict between the needs and interests of the daytime population—the workers who come into this community—and the nighttime residents. It is a conflict also between newcomers and existing residents. And finally, and perhaps most intractably, it is a conflict between those that have and those that have not; although some issues may be wrapped in concerns about density of housing and traffic congestion. There are questions of attitudes toward poverty and attitudes toward race, which set a very long agenda for More Fair. While this assessment is rather stark from the vantage point of More Fair, there is a bright side to the picture as well, namely, that those who are on the other side of this issue, the Balanced Growth people and their supporters on the city council, do not control (yet, at least) the third decisive council vote.

What should they do with the $100,000? Keep it intact as long as possible; attempt, before spending the first dollar, to have a fairly specific political and legal reconnaissance done on a volunteer basis. The group needs to understand the parameters of this particular problem on a political, legal, and social basis before it begins to fritter away what is a very small amount of money given the agenda ahead. There is some strategic value in keeping that $100,000 kitty intact as long as possible: it probably has more value as a threat to litigation in this context than what it could actually buy in services, research, canvassing, or organizing efforts.

What are the possible goals? Clearly, there must be some rezoning. The restrictive zoning in Fair City has created a situation where a very small and rather unattractive section of the city has the only multifamily housing within the city boundaries. How does it get changed? A lot has to be done to identify the pivotal third vote on the city council, what motivates him or her, what opportunities there are to influence that person and, ideally, two other members on the council. Those factors are idiosyncratic to the specific political decisionmakers, but with a little creativity More Fair will be able to find some pressure points for the three people whose support they are going to need. They are also going to need to mobilize their own supporters; failing in their effort to change public opinion, they must make felt whatever amount of support they have been able to garner in the community and must apply it in fairly focused and consistent ways.

Finally, they need to get a more concrete proposal on the table. The idea of establishing a goal of 1,200 units in the next three years is fine;

unfortunately, it is also very easily dismissed in the usual kind of political debate that occurs around such questions. They need to talk more specifically about how that goal might be accomplished. They also can be a bit more creative in expanding the boundaries of the political problem and potential legal problems with which they are confronted. If this issue were put to a vote today, or over the course of the next year or so, More Fair would lose rather convincingly. In a situation where the odds against you are fairly steep, sometimes it is strategically helpful to redefine the problem, to bring new players into the discussion, and to change the issues on which the public debate is focused.

SUSAN DESANTIS: More Fair's goal—to build 1,200 affordable apartment units in three years on scattered sites for all who work in Fair City no matter what their incomes are—may be unrealistic in light of local politics. The problems fall generally into two categories: first, the technical problems of planning and financing housing developments and second, the political problems associated with creating an environment conducive to rental housing development. Creating this environment will be More Fair's greatest challenge.

More Fair may seek to achieve its objectives either by making fuller use of the existing multifamily residential neighborhood or by seeking multifamily zoning in other parts of the city or both. Whichever direction More Fair takes, it appears to be facing opposition from a negative attitude on the part of the city staff and from a substantial no-growth constituency that may or may not represent a majority of citizens. There appears, however, to be an opportunity to develop a prohousing majority on the city council, and this is where More Fair should start.

More Fair's strategy should incorporate two elements. First, it should attempt to build a broad-based coalition for housing in the city. The Coalition should involve the areas' realtors, developers, and the building industry (including unions as well as contractors). But it should also draw in the city's employers and businesses, who have a stake in affordable housing for their lower-level employees, and in seeing that the employees' paychecks are spent within, rather than outside, the city. It should draw in potential consumers of rental housing, including senior citizens and people in their late teens and early twenties who will soon be moving from their parents' homes to apartments. The latter groups could be easily reached if Fair City contains a university or college.

Second, More Fair should seek to influence the city through direct contacts, not only at the city council level but also with the planning commission, planning staff, and advisory bodies. It should develop a participative role in city policymaking by obtaining detailed knowledge of community housing needs and of available housing resources and techniques. Using both its knowledge and its broad base of support, it will be in a position to influence prohousing decisions at all levels within the city.

The case study refers to the lack of land zoned for multifamily housing in Fair City and "the constraints of Fair City development control law and regulations." It will be difficult to change city policy on multifamily zoning. But More Fair could hope to achieve small, but significant, improvements in the housing environment through: moderate density increases in the existing multifamily area; zoning for mixed commercial and residential uses; density bonuses and fee waivers for affordable housing; reductions in the minimum lot sizes for single-family dwellings; and expedited one-stop processing with priority for affordable housing.

In addition, a planned unit development approach to zoning might be acceptable to the city because of the control over design and density the city would retain. More Fair would in this case have to continue monitoring the process to ensure that unreasonable conditions did not result in cost increases and delays.

The technical problems of developing affordable housing will be made easier by improvements in the political environment. Despite widely publicized cuts in federal housing programs, there are still many ways in which affordable housing can be built if a suitable development climate exists. It is not clear to me why the city subjected a housing bond issue to the voters: tax-exempt mortgage revenue bonds can be issued by the city without voter approval, and developers could obtain additional tax exempt financing through the California Housing Finance Agency. Rental projects with such financing fit the aims of both the city and More Fair in that they provide market rate units not subject to the stigma of public assistance while also providing affordable housing in low concentrations.

Other tools include: land banking and the use of surplus land, especially infill land; redevelopment powers and financing; community development block grant funds for financing land acquisition; and infrastructure and rehabilitation of rental housing.

The successful development of model projects, perhaps on a small scale, can be very important in impressing elected officials, city staff, and community groups with the quality and acceptability of affordable housing. For example, thoughtful, attractive design on model projects may defuse opposition to higher-density zoning.

The value of proper handling of neighborhood opposition is increasingly recognized. Efforts usually involve personal visits to homeowner groups, full disclosure of plans and design, discussion of citizen concerns, and negotiation of tradeoffs to reduce negative impacts. Some-

times a developer defeats his or her own efforts by using an unimagina-
tive, inflexible approach on a project. For example, the opposition in
Fair City to high density development may be negated by design factors.
It's not how dense you make a project that matters most—it's how you
make it dense.

Citizen opposition to affordable units in one northern California city
was substantially defused by conducting a survey of employers to determine income ranges of various employees who worked in the community
but lived outside the area because of affordability. The resulting list
included teachers, school administrators, policemen, firemen, and other
city employees. Perceptions about who occupies affordable housing were
changed in this way.

Two additional points relate to the success of federal/state/local
partnerships and the state's ability to mitigate citizen opposition to multifamily rental housing. On the first point, there are many examples of
successful projects involving cooperation and funding from all levels of
government. One of the main functions of the state's housing assistance
programs is to complement federal programs and make them easier for
local governments and developers to use.

Projects involving a number of different financing sources are difficult
and time-consuming to bring to fruition. But the projects in which the department has been involved in partnership with developers and local governments are able to add significantly to the state's affordable housing stock.

On the question of mitigating public opposition, I believe that there
is little the state would accomplish by direct intervention. In most instances interference would be counterproductive and might provoke
additional opposition. But the state can help by: developing model
projects for replication in different communities; developing and pub-
licizing acceptable approaches to affordable housing; and drawing media
attention to the current and future needs for housing in all communities
and for all economic groups. The state can also provide technical assistance to help local governments adopt policies and developers design
housing that will meet with public acceptance, and the state can support
local coalition building by groups such as More Fair.

More Fair's objectives are overly optimistic but state contributions to
mitigating public opposition cannot be effective without groups such
as More Fair. An adequate supply of affordable housing is essential for
the continued economic vitality of the state, and support for housing
at the local level from consumers, business, and advocacy groups is the
key to ensuring that supply.

V. FEI TSEN: There may be housing for low-income people, but there
is no such thing as low-cost housing. Housing is expensive to produce

compared to the amount that a low-income family can pay. Traditionally, state and federal programs have provided subsidy and loan programs that have made the production of housing possible. However, today we find significant cutbacks in federal and state support for housing development activities. The task of developing affordable housing, given the climate of funding cutbacks, has become exceedingly difficult and demands more ingenuity and innovation from the developers who remain committed to producing an affordable unit.

The developer's task is like putting together a jigsaw puzzle, except that the pieces are ever-changing. There may be only a brief point in time when the pieces can fit together. The developer must be poised to seize that opportunity.

The three major pieces of the puzzle in developing affordable housing are: (1) costs to build; (2) costs to operate; and (3) the gap between the cost of development and operation and the amount a low- or moderate-income family can afford to pay. Each of these puzzle pieces can be examined using as an example a development in Oakland.

Development Costs

The variables in the question, "What does it cost to build?", are land, construction, and soft development costs. The price of land, especially in areas experiencing fast growth, has dramatically escalated. In recent years the cost of construction in northern California has slowed, but it has still exceeded the inflation rate. Financing, permit fees, and architectural, engineering, and legal services required to put a development together, known generally as *soft* development costs, have also risen.

For an Oakland case, the total development cost was $2,300,000 for a thirty-unit development of one, two, and three-bedroom townhouse units. On an average per-unit basis, the cost was approximately $76,000 per unit. The land cost was $6,700 per unit. The construction cost was $60,000 per unit. The soft development cost was $9,300, of which over $1,000 per unit was attributed to permit and governmental fees.

Operation Costs

The largest component of the cost of operation of a housing unit is the cost of financing the development. The amount financed, the interest rate, and term all have an effect on the cost of financing. Taxes, insurance, and maintenance and management costs are other variables affecting the on-going operations cost for the owner of the housing.

Without subsidies, the rent level required to cover the costs of financing and operation on our Oakland unit is approximately $1,140 per month. A $45,600 annual household income is required to afford this unit if we use as a guide the rule that housing costs should not exceed 30 percent of household income. Obviously, even a moderate-income family could not afford the unit.

Affordability Gap

The final piece of the puzzle for the affordable housing developer is how to bridge the gap between what it costs to provide housing and how much a low- and moderate-income family can afford to pay. In our Oakland development we were able to house families whose incomes were as low as 50 percent of median income or $16,000 for a family of four. For example, for a two-bedroom unit rents ranged from $285 for very-low-income families to $490 for families with incomes at 80 percent of median.

What bag of tools does a housing developer need in order to make housing affordable to the very-low-income segment of our population? The techniques that are used to bridge the affordability gap are aimed at (1) lowering the cost of developing (land, construction, and soft costs) and thereby lowering the amount that needs to be financed and (2) lowering the cost of operation by reducing the cost of capital and the cost of management and maintenance.

In the first category are grants to write down or totally pay for the acquisition of the land, higher densities that reduce the per-unit cost of land, the lease or purchase of surplus land owned by public agencies at a lower-than-market cost, and grants to pay for a portion of construction costs. These are all actions that can be taken by public agencies for the public objective of building affordable housing for the community. Syndication is also a method used by nonprofit and for-profit developers to raise funds for a project by selling off the tax benefits to investors.

In the second category of techniques to reduce the cost of capital and operation are lower-interest loans through negotiation with financial institutions or the issuance of tax-exempt bonds. Interest subsidy or rent subsidy mechanisms have the same effect of lowering the debt service burden as do low-interest loans. Many loans by public agencies are structured on a deferred interest or deferred payment basis due upon sale, refinancing, or default. The project is then spared the burden of making debt service payments in the initial years.

No one technique will make a project affordable. Only a combination of resources and techniques will make a project viable for low- and moderate-income tenancy.

In our Oakland case study the sources that made the units affordable for very-low-income families were:

1. The city provided community development block grant (CDBG) funds for site acquisition, in effect making the land free to the project.

2. The city also provided Redevelopment Agency tax increment funds as a deferred payment loan to write down development costs. Tax increment funds are generated from increases in the tax revenue of properties located in Redevelopment Agency areas.

3. The U.S. Department of Housing and Urban Development (HUD) provided a housing development grant that was also used to write down development costs.

4. The sponsor syndicated the project and raised equity capital from limited-partner investors. The capital raised was also used to reduce the amount of development cost that needed to be financed.

5. Finally, the sponsor negotiated a low-interest loan from a local financial institution. The lender was willing to make a below-market interest rate loan as part of its community lending effort to comply with Community Reinvestment Act requirements.

The mortgage financing on the project was less than 40 percent of the total cost of the project. Grants, equity capital, and deferred payment loans made up the difference between what it cost to build the housing and what the targeted income group could afford.

The lesson to be drawn from our case study is that federal, state, and local sources of gap financing are absolutely critical for the production of new affordable housing. The developers of affordable housing must be determined and innovative about putting together a combination of techniques and resources. The major lesson for More Fair is that it is essential to get local governmental support for housing. Local government support can mean financial resources for bridging the affordability gap, tax-exempt bond financing capabilities, and fast-track processing of projects. Local government support is dependent on public support.

More Fair must then establish a coalition of support among businesses, employers, churches, and residents to push affordable housing as a priority for the community.

The reality of affordable housing development is that success is more dependent on the political will to create such housing than on the technical ability to put a development together.

HENRY FELDER: It is important to understand the federal role in housing and particularly in assisted housing for low-income and middle-income groups. We begin with the premise that the federal government has never had an active, direct role in housing for middle-income people. Neither this administration nor any previous administration has made housing an entitlement program, not even for low-income people. There has not been, except for a few selected programs, an active program of subsidies to middle-income homeowners. The cutoff line for any federal subsidy for assisted housing is 80 percent of median income. In the Fair City case the desire is to provide housing for those who have at least 80 percent of median income, up to 120 percent. So federal programs end where Fair City's problem begins.

In 1981 approximately 3.2 million low-income households were assisted through a variety of programs. By the end of this fiscal year approximately 4.1 million households will be assisted. There has been a 30 percent increase in housing assistance for low-income households since the start of this administration. How are those 4.1 million households serviced? Some of them are serviced by public housing units: 1.3 million exist across the country in the 3,200 public housing authorities that have elected to include public housing in their programs. Many local authorities, however, have decided they do not want public housing in their particular neighborhoods and jurisdictions. In that case the federal government has no role with regard to public housing. The public housing stock currently exists in a variety of conditions: disrepair, in some instances; very good repair in others. My office is currently conducting a study that will tell us exactly how much it will cost to revitalize, modernize, and repair (as needed) those 1.3 million units of public housing. The administration is committed to maintaining those 1.3 million units of public housing in a modernized and fully updated condition.

The balance of the 4.1 million households are assisted through the Section 8 New Construction Program, a very controversial program. It is the primary focus for federal government involvement in more new construction. In 1981 Section 8's share of the total HUD liability was $250 billion. Much of this had been accumulated in the period from 1974, when the New Construction Program began, until 1981; then one of the recommendations of the Commission on Housing was to cut back on further federal indebtedness for new housing. If the rate at which housing had been growing in the 1970s continued, the indebtedness for housing would soon have approached $1 trillion. In the last few years that indebtedness has decreased from $250 billion to approximately $230 billion. These are commitments by HUD for housing and for subsidies into the future. A major component of the New Construction Program was a vast transfer of wealth to, primarily, fairly affluent developers and builders. Instead of transferring funds to these groups, the administration decided it would be far better to provide vouchers and additional Section 8 certificates so that individuals could find housing in the private market. This strategy is combined with some new construction—for the elderly and for Indians—and, in instances where there are severe shortages, some spot new construction.

These assistance programs have worked very well. It has been shown that providing assistance through vouchers is the most cost-effective way to provide housing assistance for low-income people. There has been an emphasis in this administration on the worst-case household: Which household units should be serviced by assisted housing? The definition includes those whose shelters are in disrepair, whose incomes are approaching 50 percent of the median income of the community in which they reside, and who are without shelter because of a variety of circumstances. In addition to vouchers, the federal government provides for rehabilitation of privately owned rental units to become available to low-income people.

Finally, a word about the Joint Venture for Affordable Housing: there are instances in which coalitions have been formed to provide rental housing for low-income people. A very successful program was initiated in 1982, the Joint Venture for Affordable Housing. We determined that major costs of new housing construction included delays in getting permits to start construction; zoning laws that required far lower densities than necessary for health, safety, and even aesthetic reasons; and a variety of obsolete building techniques in housing construction. The Joint Venture for Affordable Housing Task Force began a process that has resulted in over forty different joint venture developments in more than thirty states. In each of these instances we have shown builders and the community that affordable housing can be aesthetically pleasing. We are seeking to undertake these demonstrations in each state in the country. The result of our efforts has been an increased awareness that requirements regarding the width of streets, the number of sidewalks, sewer lines, densities, housing materials, the amount of lumber required, and engineering have frequently been unnecessary to provide safe, decent, aesthetically pleasing, and affordable housing. In these programs there are no direct federal subsidies. Everything is done on the local level and is financed by local people.

CHRISTINE MINNEHAN: My discussion focuses on the major constraint on providing affordable rental housing—that is, you have to know how to count votes. We have all the tools here: you can file a lawsuit, design a program and get it funded, put together a proposal at the local level, help out with HUD funds for the lowest income, draft a bill for the housing committee or the judiciary committee—but if you do not have the votes, the best bill, the best program, is going to go down to indifferent defeat. Perhaps you will get two lines in the *Los Angeles Times* or an exposé in the *Sacramento Bee* or a chuckle out of your friends.

The main problem in Fair City is that there is no will to build affordable housing; there is no political leadership; and there is no percentage, to put it in rather raw terms. The case study is a study of indifference. The political and bureaucratic structures have no interest in, no constituency for, and therefore no political investment in expanding the rental housing supply. It is on this problem that I would utilize the $100,000.

The city manager clearly has thrown up his hands. A revenue bond issue would have been relatively easy. But the people have already spoken; they don't want a bond issue. Therefore, if the city is not interested in producing something, what do they do? They create a record to demonstrate that "doggone it, we really care about it, but it's just impossible to do it." Obviously, the no-growth group is a powerful group; its members live in the political jurisdiction, and they are voters, they are organizers, and they are very vocal. The city manager also makes no mention of the fact that the zoning is inconsistent with the general plan. He does point out that there are ecological constraints that do not pass CEQA review, but he did not look very far; and he did not look at the language of that law requiring a balance of housing with environmental concerns.

The 50 percent of the folks who are commuting in are not creating any political discomfort. Until they do, the political and bureaucratic (organizations) will reflect nothing more than the meaningless lip service that the city manager is providing.

The group ought to work from several sides to make the political environment uncomfortable for those who support the status quo. There are two ways I would go about that. I work for a politician, and my door is always open, but it is a lot more open to someone walking in with a solution, something I can take to Senator Roberti and say, "Here's a proposal that I think we can support and I think we can get the votes for," than it is to someone coming in and whining. If More Fair should find a hungry, creative developer to tie up a site—an entrepreneur who can cut through the red tape and get the property rezoned, get the expedited permitting, the density bonuses, all the tools that have been talked about, put together a revenue bond issue, and hire a consultant to write an environmental impact report that balances housing and environmental needs—I would bring that package to the city council. I would include industry people; they must be getting sick and tired of having 50 percent of their work force commuting. A lot of people become less dependable when they drive an hour and a half because of babysitting or car problems. You need to create within industry a positive force for affordable housing.

The $100,000 ought to be used to buy creativity. More Fair must make a positive, vote-getting, economic development environment before turning around the city council. It needs three votes! None of the other strategies is going to matter until More Fair has generated a positive vote.

RALPH CATALANO: I think the political situation in Fair City would be very easy to deal with. We have only two votes against More Fair's goal on the council, and we have a city of 200,000, which implies that the community is diverse. For some reason the city has accepted industrial development but not apartments. That sounds bizarre, but it sounds like a city that can be influenced. When we started eight years ago in Irvine, in the heart of Orange County, we had nobody on the city council supporting affordable housing; the city was known for planning and low density. Eight years later 20 percent of all new housing is affordable to moderate-income families, and a development agreement provides 2000 apartments, one-third of which must be affordable and one-third of that third must be affordable for low-income people and have three bedrooms. If you can do that in Irvine, in Orange County, without a revolution, you can do it anywhere.

Let me put my academic hat on, rather than my local government hat, for a second. This case study in some ways exemplifies what is wrong with groups like ours. We talk about a city that has an imbalance between housing and jobs. It would make more sense to look at this from a regional point of view. What is the problem? Is the problem that half of the folks who work in Fair City have to drive in? That does not mean very much as a problem. Fair City is obviously embedded in a metropolitan region, otherwise people would not be driving in. The problem is that people are working away from where they live, not that they live away from where they work. This region is attracting industrial development; Fair City is in fact growing industrially. The problem might be that other cities in this region will not accept industrial development. So the problem is finding some way to match work opportunities and housing opportunities.

To return to a local government perspective: this council can be had. Two people are against more affordable housing, but two people have said nothing, and one person is in favor. The city's general plan is blatantly violated by its zoning ordinance. If I had the $100,000, the first thing I would do is hire one damn-smart lawyer. In Irvine eight years ago we had the exact same situation. But we did not have $100,000; we had $5,000 and four or five highly motivated people. Through a series of legal entanglements we got the city to settle out of court to provide 1,400 units, not of rental housing but of for-sale housing for low- and moderate-income people. So my money would go first to a lawyer.

More Fair should warn: "This city is in trouble legally." That suddenly gives that one person on the council legitimacy to influence the two others who are hanging back. Those two people can then come out and say, "Look, I ordinarily wouldn't support this, but good lord, the legal battle will cost so much money, it will get so messy, and in the end we're going to lose, so I'd rather go out and negotiate now and get the best deal we can get."

The city has accepted industrial development; so More Fair is not faced with a group of rabid environmentalists who are opposed to any kind of threatening physical changes. Residential development can certainly be made acceptable. Whether this city has a great deal of undeveloped property or very little undeveloped property, there are ways around this factor.

The political problem is not severe in this town; the financial gap makes the problem. But if the gap is not a problem, Fair City could get this housing.

Let me make a connection between the academic perspective on this and the issue of politics. It is in the economic interest of communities to make it possible to provide moderately priced rental housing. A compelling economic case can be made that we need moderately priced housing, particularly rental housing. In Orange County we have tried hard to make that case for the last five years. The recently completed fifth annual survey of Orange County households revealed that 44 percent want more rental housing in Orange County, and 59 percent of those respondents said that they are willing to use the public sector to make rental housing available. We have made the argument that if we are going to be happy people, we need to have a firm economic base; to have a firm economic base we need a diverse labor force; and to have a diverse labor force in a region, we need a diverse housing stock. In Orange County we can point out housing that is for moderate- and low-income families and demonstrate that it is not unattractive housing.

Resistance to programs such as More Fair's may be based on the experience of ten years ago. Things have changed.

JOHN DANNER: I agree that there is nothing other than a lawsuit or the gallows that seems to focus people's attention; my concern is that people get into a litigation posture too soon, before they have figured out what it is they want to get done and have identified the most vulnerable pressure point for applying that litigation. I have seen groups who assume that a lawsuit is going to be the solution to their problem, when in fact it is more often a way to focus people's attention.

Second, I would like to touch briefly on a model in San Francisco called the Office/Affordable Housing Production Program (OAHPP). It is an effort by the city, recently enacted in ordinance form, to link the attendant social costs of downtown office development to housing by asking office developers of projects over 50,000 square feet to contribute to the housing stock of low- and moderate-units. They do this in one of three ways. As the price of getting a temporary certificate of occupancy for those downtown office buildings, developers are obligated to either pay about five dollars per square foot into a housing production fund; construct housing on the site of their development, 62 percent of which must meet the ordinance's definition of low- and moderate-income-affordable units; or do some combination of the two. It is a fairly novel and controversial approach. There are questions about its effectiveness, but most people conclude that substantial numbers of housing units in San Francisco would not have been there but for this particular program.

PANELIST QUESTION: Do you see replication of that model anywhere but in San Francisco, a highly desirable area? If you were to say "let's do that in Fresno" or "let's do that in El Centro," would it work there?

JOHN DANNER: It is replicable, but it may be replicable only in San Francisco-type situations. For example, Boston has a program called the Linkage Program, which is presently less stringent than San Francisco's. But you do have generically similar circumstances there. It is difficult to see whether Fair City is that much of a mecca. To the extent that it is a mecca and people do want to locate new office or new industrial plants there, that model is another means to create some money to close the financial gap that we have discussed.

HENRY FELDER: In addition to the stick of litigation, I think there is a lot to be said about the carrot of friendly persuasion. In many instances people are unaware of what constitutes affordable housing, either rental housing or ownership housing. There is a misconception that when you say affordable housing, you mean cheap housing where adjacent housing values will go down; there are all sorts of unfair negative stereotypes that surround the idea of bringing in housing that costs less than existing housing does. The Joint Venture Program aims to inform people about how aesthetically pleasing affordable housing can be, and about what it means to the community to provide housing that will support such households as new professionals, schoolteachers, and the service workers who in many instances are priced out of that community. In addition to using the threat of litigation, Fair City should spend a fair amount of its efforts educating and seeking models of affordability that are pleasing and beneficial to the community.

FAY TSEN: The first thing that we do is work with the neighborhood because we know that we cannot put a development through unless we have neighborhood support. Neighborhood support assists in getting the techniques to reduce development costs—like fee waivers and land write-downs.

There is an image of low-income housing, affordable housing, that is like the 1950s or 1960s public housing. The type of nonprofit-sponsored housing being built now is very attractive; it is housing for people of moderate income; and in San Francisco moderate income means $36,000 per year. In some of the bond programs, the housed people earn $50,000 annually. That income range includes most of us: the middle class, teachers, nurses, college professors, and bankers. That point needs to be made: More Fair must educate the neighborhoods and the city as to what affordable housing means.

RALPH CATALANO: A point was made earlier that the city staff in Fair City is a problem. But most city staffs know where their paychecks come from. If the city council made it clear that something must be done, it would get done. City managers are professionals who very rarely allow their personal values to intercede in a case like this.

AUDIENCE COMMENT: I have a bit of advice for More Fair: not to become too parochial. Look closely at the role of the public sector both at the state and the federal level. For some projects, more than half of the funding comes from a public source. So to develop affordable housing we have to look at how we are going to be creative enough to get funding. We can apply a variety of new proposals, but we have to have a substantial commitment from the public sector to make anything happen.

AUDIENCE QUESTION: When it was suggested that higher density can help housing affordability, has it not been found that up-zoning property simply drives up the price of the land indirectly?

RALPH CATALANO: We've seen that happen in Orange County. You almost have to adjust density on a case-by-case basis after the entitlement. You will still have a speculative effect. The possibility of density change will drive up the land price and take away some of the advantage. By the way, there is not a lot of onus to go from twelve units an acre, which is what they have in Fair City, to sixteen, where these things start to "pencil." It is not as if you are giving away a great deal. In suburban southern California, the trouble with increased density is not its social stigma or its aesthetics; the trouble is really the traffic effect. There is no way around it; increased density has an infrastructure effect.

7

Rental Housing Regulation in California: What Do We Know?

Michael B. Teitz*

Introduction: Rent Control as an Issue

Rent control, the regulation of rent levels and associated aspects of private rental housing, is a powerful issue that often generates political passion. The debate occurs at the local, state, and federal levels of government and in the executive, legislative, and judicial branches. At different periods the focus may be at one or another of these, but, over time, arguments have been carried from local city councils to the U.S. Supreme Court. For many people much is at stake in the regulation of rent levels for housing, and it is difficult to discuss the issue in a temperate way. Nevertheless, there has been a substantial number of studies, albeit mixed in quality, and some light can be shed on a number of the central questions.

The purpose of this paper is to review some of those questions and to indicate what is known and what is not. Before doing that, however, it will be helpful first to trace some of the development of rental regulation in the United States and to identify its key elements.

Rental Regulation in California: Its Origins and Extent

The origins of rent control in California are to be found in national emergencies, primarily in World Wars I and II. In the latter especially, the redirection of resources resulted in a sharp decrease in housing

*Department of City and Regional Planning, U. of California, Berkeley, Calif.

production at the same time as increases in demand occurred owing to war related development. The result was an attempt to freeze rents at their existing levels in an emergency framework, with little attention to longer-term needs or consequences, since regulation was expected to be no more than temporary. In fact, rental regulation was abolished after 1945 virtually everywhere except in New York City. Nonetheless, the precedent had been established and would not be forgotten.

More recently, regulation reemerged in the United States in 1969 with the adoption by New York City of the first of what have come to be called second generation rent controls. Such controls are often formally termed *rent stabilization*, such as in Los Angeles, but the older terminology remains in general use, and I will employ it here. This rebirth of rent control incorporated an element that has been visible in many subsequent instances. Rather than any major external crisis being identified as the justification for rental regulation, control was instituted in response to a sharp upward move in rents in part of the local housing market. In the face of local political pressure from tenants who saw themselves not only paying more rent but also possibly being forced to move in response to large rent increases, cities have adopted ordinances that regulate rent increases and many other aspects of the housing market.

The example of New York City was repeated throughout the 1970s, with both external and local factors involved in the decisions to institute control. Inflation, first in the Nixon-era oil price shock and subsequent price controls and later in the inflationary response to the sharp oil price increases of the late 1970s, has been an obvious factor. In California the passage of the property tax limitation measure, Proposition 13, also mobilized outraged renters when owners failed to pass through some of the tax savings promised during the campaign. But in each instance controls were adopted at the local rather than the state level, indicating that it was the local impact of these and other more geographically specific influences that gave rise to irresistible political pressures. New Jersey and New York have passed enabling legislation, but in California, neither pro- nor antirent control forces have been able to pass statewide legislation.[1]

Throughout this process rent control has changed in character. As it spread from New York City into other states, notably New Jersey and California, which have more rent-controlled cities than any other states, rent control has matured through a process of judicial challenge and political adjustment to become quite diverse. Court challenges have made clear the necessity for inclusion of provision for an adequate mechanism for rents to rise in order to avoid the charge that a control ordinance is confiscatory. Similarly, owners have been allowed to increase rents to make capital improvements and, in some instances, to raise rents to market levels upon vacancy. This flexibility has led some observers to use the term *moderate rent control* for all regulation that does not conform to the original stringent form. The term is useful, but its use should be more discriminating.

How extensive is rent control, in whatever form? Nationwide, there are about 128 cities with some significant form of regulation, accounting for perhaps 10 percent of total rental housing units. In California thirteen cities control rents on standard residential units; many more regulate rents for mobile home sites. Over 35 percent of all rental housing units are subject to some form of regulation. This is not a trivial percentage, and any significant change implies substantial gains and losses to the interest groups involved. Thus it is important to understand the elements of a rent control system and how they affect the outcome for landlords and tenants.

Key Elements in Rental Regulation Systems

Rent control ordinances do very greatly, both in their intent and in their specific organizational structures, rules, and operations. Each of these factors is important in shaping the outcome of regulation for the various groups that participate in the housing market.

Price regulation in market economies, of which rent control is a variant, has generally had three broad purposes: first, prevention of the exaction of excess profits by holders of natural monopolies, such as telephones and utilities; second, mitigation of the effects of market fluctuations that result in inequitable prices of consumer necessities during periods of shortage, for example, famines; and third, prevention of ruinous competition among producers during periods of glut or economic difficulty, such as the Great Depression. Rent control is generally enacted for the second of these purposes and is therefore usually seen as a temporary measure. However, among advocates of nonmarket allocation of necessities, it is often seen as a long-term means of insulating housing from the more general market economy, especially for the poor. The long-term goal of these advocates is changing the system of property relations. It is important to bear in mind the various forms of intent if we are to understand the politics and outcomes of conflicts over rent control and the attitudes of those participating in them.

The rules and organizational structures under which rent control may operate are equally diverse and also deeply affect the outcomes. The logic of regulation in a market system, however, does require some key elements. To appreciate how rent control systems function, it is necessary to understand these elements and their interactions.

Most visible and politically volatile are rent-setting mechanisms, which determine permissible adjustments to rent and are necessary to avoid legal challenges to regulatory ordinances on confiscatory grounds. If an ordinance has a timely and equitable landlord hardship appeal mechanism, then a general rent adjustment procedure is not strictly necessary. In practice, however, most localities have some form of citywide rent adjustment to reflect changing costs of operation in a way that does not require time-consuming administrative processes. Such measures vary widely, from adjustments that simply reflect general price inflation (the Consumer Price Index) to pass-throughs of specific cost increases, such as those for fuel oil in the 1970s. In addition rents may be raised in a number of other ways, for example, by allowing owners to establish market rents on vacancy (usually called vacancy decontrol) and allowing rent increases to reflect expenditures on capital improvements. The basis for most forms of rent adjustment is to allow owners to continue to realize an adequate rate of return on their investments in rental property, which has led to a long-standing and indeterminate debate about the definition of such a rate of return.[2]

An axiom of price regulation is that it cannot be effective unless the supply of the regulated commodity is also controlled. In the absence of supply regulation black markets rapidly develop and negate the price control. In rental housing security of tenure and maintenance of quality are the counterparts of rental regulation. The most prevalent form of supply regulation is the enactment of a requirement that eviction can occur only for a limited set of just-cause reasons, most notably nonpayment of rent. In effect the tenant is given an indefinite lease. Supplementary forms of regulation also become necessary as owners seek to take advantage of market conditions and find ways to increase their returns legally. Primary among these are limitations on an owner's ability to reduce services without a comparable decrease in rents and regulation of the nature and quantity of capital improvements that may be made and charged for without the tenant's consent.

On a larger scale owners' attempts to avoid regulation by shifting their investments often result in controls on the conversion of property to other uses or legal forms. Such controls have focused especially on condominium conversion, but they commonly also cover demolition and replacement of rental housing for other uses, such as offices. From the opposite perspective, the fear that investment in rental housing will be inhibited by controls has led to the exemption of rental housing constructed after the adoption of regulation.

Finally, rent regulation requires an organization and system to carry it out. Governance of the system is critical, raising the questions of whether control will rest with an elected or appointed group and how the system will be managed and financed. The rules and operations of the system may be very complex and extensive. Among the key issues that must be determined are the definition of exactly which types of property will be regulated, whether owners must register buildings or units, whether enforcement will occur through inspection or on demand, and what will be the priorities for dealing with appeals. All of these together will reflect the spirit with which regulation is implemented, whether it favors one side or the other, and whether its objectives are limited or broad.

This adds up to a much more complex view of rent control than that typically offered by its advocates or its opponents. Regulation is never universal in its effects. It may favor either producers or consumers, and its outcomes may differ in the short and longrun. To assess its effects requires careful analysis of outcomes in specific conditions with particular forms of regulation, rather than theoretical or ideological incantations. Such analyses are beginning to be carried out, although still few in number, and we can turn to them for some clues as to reality.

What Do We Know About Rent Control?

For all the words written on the subject, hard information on the nature and effects of rent control is hard to find. The following observations do not claim to be exhaustive; rather they highlight some areas of interest and concern on the topic of rental regulation in the United States.

First, there are substantial differences among ordinances, including the important distinctions noted above between first- and second-generation controls and more importantly between moderate and restrictive second-generation controls. Few studies have really examined the differences, although Baar (1983) explored the range of variation in regulations, and Gupta and Rea (1984) attempted to explore differences systematically for cities in California. Some authors, notably Gilderbloom (1980, 1983) have tended to blur the distinction, equating all post-1969 ordinances with moderate control. More careful analysis linking specific elements of different systems to their outcomes is called for.

The most basic questions on rent control ultimately concern rent levels. What kinds of effects have controls had on rent levels where they have been implemented? Are average rent levels held down? Are some types of buildings, owners, and tenants favored, while others are penalized? Despite the obviousness of the questions, surprisingly little research has been done on them. The evidence suggests that average rent levels may have been held down in California only in a minority of cities with quite restrictive ordinances, notably Berkeley and Santa Monica. For moderate versions of control, the evidence from the *1984 Los Angeles Rental Housing Study* (1985a) suggests that average rents after six years of control were not significantly different from those in surrounding cities without rent control. Analyses of New Jersey by Gilderbloom (1984) and New York State by Vitaliano (1983) tend to find similar outcomes.

If controls often do not lower rents on the average, what do they do? First, they provide increased security of tenure for tenants in the face of shifts in housing submarkets. If, for whatever reason, substantially higher rents become economically feasible in a particular market, landlords are prevented from either extracting them from sitting tenants or evicting those tenants in favor of tenants able and willing to pay more. How long such an effect may last is questionable. The incentives for owners to find other means of realizing the potential gains by reducing services and maintenance, by inducing tenants to leave by legal or illegal means, or by changing the legal forms of property have been pointed out by advocates and opponents of control alike. A major source of contention in rent control disputes is the extent of such behavior. At this time we simply do not know. It seems likely that this too varies widely among jurisdictions and rent control systems.

Besides providing security of tenure, at least to the extent allowed by the particular system, rent control seems to provide distinct advantages to selected groups of tenants. The most obviously advantaged group comprises tenants with substantial longevity of tenure. In Los Angeles virtually all estimated financial benefits flowed to tenants who had occupied their apartments since before the adoption of the rent stabilization ordinance.[3] For them, the benefits were not trivial, averaging between $47 and $55 per month, or 2 to 3 percent of income. These tenants were more often of moderate or low income, though many were not, and they were more likely to be white, elderly, or members of single-person households. Other tenants received little monetary benefit, and indeed some of them appeared to be paying substantially more than they might have done in the absence of control. A recent study in New York City comes to similar conclusions. Thus it is not clear that rent control unambiguously favors tenants, even if we ignore the longer-term questions of its effects on supply.

The opposite side of the coin is the effect of controls on the economic viability of rental housing and the consequent impacts on investment in supply of existing and new units. Several different issues have been debated for many years, but firm evidence on any of them is hard to come by. They include impacts on profitability of operation, on levels of maintenance and capital investment in the existing stock, and on investment in construction of new rental housing.

The obstacles to measurement of rates of return on investment in rental housing are formidable. Owners are reluctant to provide accurate data that include the tax consequences of investments. Even with such data, the variation in owners' economic goals makes inference difficult.[4] On the basis of their universally fierce opposition it seems safe to say that owners perceive controls as reducing the profitability of rental housing ownership. Exactly how large the reduction might be or who bears it is much less clear. Rent control advocates often point to the fact that such lost profits may be attributable primarily to short-term inability of housing markets to respond to sudden shifts in demand, and they are therefore, in economic terms, *scarcity rents*, not necessary for long-term investment to occur. Opponents argue that the cyclical nature of housing production is such that swings from glut to scarcity regularly occur and that this year's rent increase may offset last year's premium. Neither side considers the potential advantages to owners of long-term stability allied with scarcity.

The Los Angeles study experienced the usual difficulties in obtaining sufficient data from owners of rental housing, but it did supplement survey data with information from other sources, especially property sales and state income tax data. The results therefore may have a greater robustness than others that depend solely on surveys. The data suggest that in this case of a moderate regulatory system, rates of return have not been significantly lowered—a result that is quite consistent with the finding that average rents are comparable to those in cities without rent control. In the initial period following the adoption of rent stabilization by the city, rates of return appear to have fallen quite sharply relative to the comparison cities. In later years, however, returns exceeded those in noncontrolled areas. Why this occurred is open to speculation. The latter result may well have occurred as a consequence of low levels of vacancy and the growing awareness by investors that the system was being operated in a way that did not primarily favor either landlords or tenants.

This is not to suggest that such consequences are universal. Both theory and some evidence suggest that stringent controls do reduce profitability, especially for owners who are in place when controls come into force. What is important is that the outcome will depend on the circumstances of regulation, just as it does in other regulated industries.

How does rent control affect maintenance and reinvestment in the existing housing stock? Again, the evidence is quite scanty—first, because the problem has not been extensively studied and second, because the task of measuring change in housing quality is immensely difficult. Economic theory is quite clear on this subject; a rational owner would have a clear incentive to reduce maintenance and defer improvements in the face of rental reduction. However, theory tells us nothing about the level of regulation necessary to induce a response that is measurable or how fast it would occur. Given the modest impact on rents, the scale of effect in many instances may not be within our means to detect it. That seems to be the case in Los Angeles, where most indicators of housing quality fell after rent control, but the decline was even greater in noncontrolled cities. Other studies, such as those by Eckert (1977), Vitaliano (1983), and Wolfe (1983), fail to document declines in maintenance. Rydell's (1981) rather elegant model of the process led him to the conclusion that the predicted level of quality in Los Angeles would decline at a rate of 1 to 2 percent per year, much slower than most people might have expected. Nonetheless, the subjective sense of physical deterioration in cities with stringent controls is very strong. This topic needs much more work.

If maintenance has been little studied, the effects of rent control on capital improvements have been even less so. Again, the difficulty of finding appropriate data appears to be critical. Furthermore, the data that do exist tend to be affected by the fact that most jurisdictions allow rents to be increased with some capital improvements. Landlords are thereby given an incentive for investment that has more to do with the nature of the regulatory system than with the market.

Finally, the questions of impact on new construction, conversion, demolition, and abandonment have been among the most fiercely debated in rent control. The theoretical presumption is clear that a reduction in price should inhibit new supply. However, since most ordinances exempt newly constructed housing from rental regulation, rent control's impact occurs only through the mechanism of its effect on anticipations by investors. In rental housing that means developers, lenders, and other investors—both individuals and institutions. For a developer, the real issue may concern not so much the existence of rent control as its specific rules and whether those rules may be taken as stable over the period necessary for an adequate rate of return to be realized.

The Los Angeles (1985b) study is consistent with studies of other moderate-rent-control localities, especially Gilderbloom (1980, 1983), in finding little impact on new construction. That may be due in part to the difficulty of detecting an effect during a period of great turmoil in the housing market with huge swings in interest rate levels. I suspect, however, that it is also due to the adjustment of expectations to the rent control environment, which in Los Angeles has been rightly seen as quite stable. If developers and lenders perceive no change over several years, that is, close to the effective investment horizon, then they will simply discount the modest additional risk along with other elements of uncertainty in their investment calculations.

So far as it is possible to tell from the Los Angeles data, there may well have been a downward shift in new private rental housing in the city relative to noncontrolled comparison areas immediately around the time when rent stabilization was adopted. By 1985, however, the relative level of new construction was greater in Los Angeles than in the comparison cities. I would not necessarily attribute this to the existence of rent control, but it certainly does not suggest any major negative impact after several years.

Demolitions and conversions are in many respects parallel issues to new construction. Conversion ordinances have been adopted almost everywhere that rent control exists, indicating strong local perceptions that the opportunity to escape regulation will be taken by owners able to do so. The level and rate of condominium conversions, however, does not solely depend upon regulation of rents. It is also deeply affected by the general level of demand in the housing market and by supply of single-family homes. There is room for much more work to assess the relationship here. Much the same may be said for demolitions. Virtually no systematic studies of demolitions in relation to rent control have been done. Kirlin's brief study of Santa Monica suggests that demolitions rose sharply in anticipation of the passage of rent control. But that case was one in which the level of political rhetoric was unusually high, and the anticipation of stringent controls was justified.

I have deliberately given little attention to one of the most heated issues in rent control debates, namely, its effect on the abandonment of rental housing. This absence is due to the fact that there is no abandonment to speak of in California. I believe that there are circumstances in which rent control can and does contribute to abandonment, but they are not present in California at this time. Other important issues also exist, most notably the effect of rental regulation on the property tax base. At this point I doubt that sufficient evidence exists to be able to relate such effects to particular forms and levels of rent control.

Political and Social Aspects of Rent Control

Although the consequences of rent control seem often to be quite modest, few people would deny that it is a political issue that can stir up strong emotions. Yet one looks in vain for careful analyses of the political processes involved or the political consequences that result. Much the same can be said for social outcomes. Nevertheless, my experience and observation suggest that some important political and social characteristics do emerge where rent control becomes an issue. We see noisy and bitter conflicts, great difficulty in reaching compromises, political polarization, unexpected coalitions, and unstable alliances. Where it is established, rent control also tends to become a long-term issue. Such outcomes are not always present, and indeed careful studies may show that I am reacting largely to a few instances, such as New York City, where this scenario is characteristic. Yet I feel that this is at least a widely held perception of the nature of the rent control phenomenon, and we need to examine it and ask why these characteristics seem to occur.

A simple interpretation would see only a conflict of interest over financial gain, but that is insufficient to account for the depth of feeling and bitterness that is often involved. I believe instead that there is a fundamental asymmetry of perceptions and expectations between the principal participants in debates over rent control.

Consider the landlord and tenant views of the housing and rent situation in a tight housing market. The property-owner sees rent control as imposing a real financial loss, namely, the difference between the rent that could be set for a housing unit and the rent that is being actually realized. Although the estimate of the prospective rent may be too large owing to false expectations, there is no doubt that some increase would be possible, often a substantial one. The tenant, on the other hand, knows that he or she is occupying the same unit as before, with no change in quality, only the prospect of a higher price. Awareness of rising rents in the market may give a sense of increased value, especially to sophisticated tenants, but to others, such as the elderly, it may simply bring anxiety. So the perceptions of the parties involved as to the value of what is being debated are profoundly different. Add to this the size of housing payments in a typical household budget, together with the importance of the house as a psychological element of emotional stability, and the ingredients of a powerful conflict are clearly present.

In a certain sense there is a parallel dissimilarity in perception between neoclassical economists and housing activists who tend to play out the rent control conflict in the political-economic arena. Economists are almost universally opposed to rent control, seeing its negative effects principally in terms of behavior in their theoretical model and being concerned with market efficiency and aggregate outcomes. Activists, on the other hand, see that unfettered changes in the market entail heavy burdens for people who have few resources and have done nothing to bring them about. They care little about long-term market effects, often denying their existence. The possibility of mobilizing tenants as resources for a larger political struggle may contribute to this view. Again, there is little common ground on which the two can meet.

Beyond the asymmetry of perceptions there is also an asymmetry in meaning and expectations. It is not simply a question of costs and benefits but of what rent control means to each side. To landlords, I think that it is clear that rent control means an attack on private property. Whether that will change with the experience of moderate regulation is doubtful. We are unlikely to see advocacy of regulation by owners of rental housing to prevent ruinous competition, as has occurred in other sectors. For advocates, the meaning may vary from benign regulation all the way to the sense that this is a vehicle with which fundamental property relations in society may be overturned. My sense is that most tenants are not interested in the latter, which may be one reason why advocates have a difficult time building stable, radical coalitions on the basis of rent control. There is a tendency to build a coalition nominally to achieve many objectives, but after rent control is achieved, the coalition falls apart because the rest of the program is not really attractive. I suspect that this happened in Santa Monica.

In sum, there are many interesting political and social outcomes of rent control. We find coalitions, for example, of the elderly, environmentalists, historic preservationists, and radicals. We find unstable alliances that last a while and then fall apart. We find political fragmentation and polarization, especially if an elected rent board becomes independent of local government; Berkeley may be a good example of that. We find the emergence of new, entrenched interest groups—what Montgomery (1985) following Gouldner calls the new class—that are sufficiently affluent and politically adept to be able to appropriate property value from owners through a political process that emphasizes environmental or other qualities of neighborhoods.

Conclusion

Rent control is more than simple regulation of the price of a commodity. It carries with it a range of meanings that give rise to passionately held views and often extreme rhetoric. Yet, despite the claims, rent control is no more monolithic than any other form of regulation. In the U.S. context it is much less so than most other forms. Although we know more about it than was the case a few years ago, we still do not fully understand how different forms and degrees of regulation actually affect the outcomes for the participants. The battle may continue to rage even if we do gain that understanding, but I suspect that there may come to be a larger common ground upon which the issues can be brought to mutually acceptable resolutions.

Notes

1. Perhaps the best survey of rent control legislation and judicial decisions in recent years is Baar (1983). An excellent survey of rent control in California is Keating (1983).
2. For a good review of this issue see Baar (1983).
3. See Los Angeles (1985a).
4. Wolfe (1983) provides one of the few studies to document this point.

References

Baar, Kenneth (1983). "Guidelines for Drafting Rent Control Laws: Lessons of a Decade." *Rutgers Law Review* 35(4): 721–885.

Eckert, Joseph (1977). "The Effect of Rent Control on Assessment Policies, Differential Incidence of Taxation, and Income Adjustment Mechanisms for Rental Housing in Brookline, Massachusetts." Medford, Mass.: Tufts University, Ph.D. Dissertation.

Gilderbloom, John (1983). "The Impact of Moderate Rent Control in New Jersey: An Empirical Study of 26 Rent Controlled Cities." *Urban Analysis* 7(2): 135–154.

——— (1981). "Moderate Rent Control: Its Impact on the Quality and Quantity of the Housing Stock." *Urban Affairs Quarterly*, 17(2): 123–142.

——— (1980). *Moderate Rent Control: The Experience of U.S. Cities.* Washington, D.C.: Conference on Alternative State and Local Public Policies, Policy Report No. 3.

Gupta, Dipka and L. Rea (1984). "Second Generation Rent Control Ordinances: A Quantitative Comparison." *Urban Affairs Quarterly.* 19(3): 395–408.

Keating, Dennis (1983). *Rent Control in California: Responding to the Housing Crisis.* Berkeley, Calif.: University of California, Berkeley, Institute of Governmental Studies.

Los Angeles (1985a). *The Los Angeles Rent Stabilization System: Impacts and Alternatives.* Report prepared by Hamilton, Rabinovitz, Szanton, and Alschuler. Los Angeles: Community Development Department, Rent Stabilization Division.

—— (1985b). *Housing Production and Market Performance Under Rent Stabilization.* Report prepared by Rent Stabilization Division. Los Angeles: Community Redevelopment Department, Rent Stabilization Division.

Montgomery, Roger (1985). "Interpreting Gentrification Case Studies: A Perspective." *Journal of Urban and Contemporary Law* 28: 241–48.

Rydell, C. Peter et al. (1981). *The Impact of Rent Control on the Los Angeles Housing Market.* Santa Monica, Calif.: The Rand Corporation.

Vitaliano, Donald F. (1983). "The Economic Consequences of Rent Control: Some Evidence from New York City." Paper presented at the 1983 colloquium on rent control. Cambridge, Mass.: Lincoln Institute of Land Policy.

Wolfe, Marian F. (1983). "The Actual and Perceived Profitability in Rental Housing: A Disaggregate Analysis." Berkeley, Calif.: University of California, Berkeley, Ph.D. Dissertation.

8

The Los Angeles Rent Stabilization Program: Update 1985

*Francine F. Rabinovitz**

The Backdrop for the Rent Stabilization Program

In 1978 Californians attempted to decrease what they perceived as excessively high property taxes by passing Proposition 13, a $7 billion property tax cutting measure. At the time some citizens felt this measure would help decrease housing costs not only in the single-family home-owner market but also for renters, since when landlord tax payments were reduced such reductions would be passed on to renters. Howard Jarvis, the father of Proposition 13, along with coauthor Paul Gann, publicly argued that tenants would get significant rent reductions if the proposition passed. Indeed, just prior to passage the California Apartment Owners Association announced that its members would agree to give a 50 percent rebate on the end-of-year rental payments of their tenants if the proposition passed. At the time 57.4 percent of the population of the city of Los Angeles was composed of renters, who paid an average rent of $166 in current dollars and spent an average of 28 percent of their incomes on rent. Only 2.5 percent of the existing rental units were vacant.[1]

When a Los Angeles city council committee investigated what was occurring in the months following the passage of the proposition, they discovered that 11 percent of renters had received increases after the

The study on which this paper reports was prepared by Hamilton, Rabinovitz, Szanton, and Alschuler in association with the Urban Institute under contract to the city of Los Angeles Rent Stabilization Division.
*University of Southern California, Los Angeles, Calif.

proposition went into effect. Eleven per cent of landlords had frozen rents, and an additional 7 percent of landlords had passed through a part of their tax savings. Most of the increases were occurring in the central and south-central areas of the city. In August, 1978, the committee recommended and the council adopted a rent rollback and freeze to place rents at their May 31, 1978, preproposition level. On March 15, 1979, the city council enacted and the Mayor signed into law the city's first rent control ordinance since World War II.[2]

The Design of the Ordinance

Every rental dwelling in the city is covered by the ordinance, including mobile homes and mobile home pads, except for single-family dwellings, luxury rentals,[3] hotels, new buildings,[4] commercial and industrial property, and public housing. After May, 1979, rent increases automatically occur only if the rental unit had not had an increase in twelve months, at the rate of 7 percent per year, one year after the last rent increase. If a rental unit is voluntarily vacated by all its tenants, the landlord can raise the rent to any amount for a subsequent tenant. If the unit is removed from the market for repairs, the landlord can raise the rent any amount when the unit is available again. Rents can also be raised to the market level if the unit is vacated for just cause.

The ordinance also contains provisions for evictions if the tenant fails to pay the rent, violates conditions of tenancy, or refuses access. The landlord can remove the unit from the market for demolition or major repairs or to rent it to members of his immediate family.[5] In this case the tenant can be evicted and the unit decontrolled until the next unrelated tenant moves in. The landlord can also raise the rent when he makes capital improvements or rehabilitates the building but only with city approval.[6]

All rental units covered have to be registered by the landlord, who must pay a $3 per-unit registration fee that covers the costs of running the program.

By 1982 tenant groups were aware that the 7 percent rent increase permitted by the ordinance was in excess of the then current rate of inflation. The changed economic climate spurred demands for a policy decision to change the ordinance. In November 1983, when the program had been in effect for four years, the mayor and council directed the Rent Stabilization Division (RSD) of the Department of Community Development to look at the impact of the program with an eye to providing the basis for adjusting the maximum annual rent increase for units permitted under the ordinance. They also asked RSD to consider possible alternative methods for directing the benefits of rent stabilization to low-income and senior citizen tenants. Working with a steering committee composed of representatives of property-owners, tenant groups, organized labor, and other parties, each of whom had a technical advisor selected by the group but paid by the city, the division subsequently devised a carefully crafted request for proposals, reviewed the bids received, and in September 1984 awarded a study contract. The division elected to perform the new construction and housing market performance aspect of the study internally. The findings reported below are derived from that work and include data of both the work performed in-house and that performed by the consultants.[7] The study concluded in general that in many crucial areas there is no evidence that the city's stabilization program has made any measurable difference in the evolution of the rental housing market. The specific meaning of this finding for tenants, apartment owners, and the pattern of new construction and reinvestment is detailed below.

Tenant Experience under Rent Stabilization in Los Angeles

There are about 1.3 million tenants in some 489,000 rental units in the housing stock. A good starting point for thinking about tenants is to note that despite the heated political debate that always occurs when controls are discussed, about two out of five tenants in Los Angeles did not know in 1984 whether or not their dwellings were subject to rent stabilization. Intensive examination of the tenant experience indicates that rent stabilization in Los Angeles has had little effect on the average rate of increase in rents, including utility costs, paid by city tenants as compared with those in cities contiguous to Los Angeles practicing no form of rent regulation.[8] The average rate of increase in the city during the period since stabilization was enacted has been 10.9 percent per year, compared to 11.1 percent in surrounding unstabilized areas. The difference represents well under 1 percent of the income of tenants in stabilized units.

When this difference between average stabilized and unstabilized rents is converted into savings on monthly rent bills, it translates into a modest seven dollars per month per household. Put another way, the evidence indicates that under the Los Angeles form of rent control only very modest subsidies have flowed from all landlords to all tenants. Tenants perceive a much greater benefit. They estimate that the benefit they receive is from seven to twenty times higher than the benefit actually received.

Nevertheless, sizable subsidies do in fact flow to some types of tenants. The analysis indicates that these subsidies are financed in part by other tenants who pay premiums above what their rents would be if stabilization had not been enacted. The most important determinant of which tenants are subsidized and which pay premiums is the length of time that a household has remained in its rental unit. If the household has not moved at all since enactment of rent stabilization, the subsidy averages $47 to $55 per month. If the household moved during the 1982–1983 period, the study indicates it paid an average premium of $15 to $28 per month more in rent than it would have been charged for the same unit if rent stabilization had not been adopted.

The primary vehicle for the subsidy flow is the markup charged to an incoming tenant renting a vacant apartment. Since the rent stabilization ceiling on increases charged to tenants who do not vacate was 7 percent, the only means by which average rents can keep up with average unstabilized rents in the metropolitan area is to make the markups on vacated units much higher. The average markup in the city in 1984 was approximately 14 percent, and markups in 1982 and 1983, when double digit inflation was a reality, were much greater.

Particular sets of demographic characteristics are associated with long- and short-tenured households. Those who have stayed in their units longest tend to be smaller households, of low-to-moderate income, housed in smaller buildings, composed of older members, and less often comprised of members of a racial/ethnic minority than households that have moved. The net overall effect of stabilization has been to permit between 12,000 and 25,000 households in the city to keep their housing costs lower than the standard measure of affordability, that is, 30 to 40 percent of total household income.

The Impact of Stabilization on Landlords in Los Angeles

The 489,000 stabilized rental housing units in the city of Los Angeles are located on 70,000 properties. Over the entire period of stabilization to 1984, the financial experience of the owners of these properties was only slightly less remunerative on the average than that of owners of unstabilized properties in contiguous areas. That result was not achieved smoothly, however. The rates of return to landlords in the years immediately following enactment of stabilization dipped notice-ably. In recent years, however, returns have been increasing at higher rates than in surrounding areas so that the average net financial effect on owners who have held onto their properties throughout the period has been modest.

One important aspect of the owner experience is whether Los Angeles owners are under greater financial pressure in operating buildings than owners outside the city. The national average for operating-expense-to-income ratios in the apartment industry suggests that expenses generally represent 44 to 47 percent of income. Los Angeles landlords under stabilization were operating below this ratio, although operating costs appeared to be a slightly larger fraction of building income in the city than in surrounding areas. Operating expenses fell from 1977 to 1983, from about 49 percent in the first year to about 40 percent in 1983. The key reason was Proposition 13, which produced a 45 percent decline in tax expense and more than offset the continuing increases in other expense categories.

The Behavior of Construction and Reinvestment under Rent Stabilization

The behavior of rental housing construction and reinvestment during the rent stabilization period followed the same general profile as landlord finance. Total new construction fell in the city by almost two-thirds during the period 1978–1982 and then rebounded sharply to a new peak in 1984. Capital improvements were sustained, although those supported by rent increases specially granted under the terms of the stabilization ordinance itself have been concentrated in the larger build-ings. While one must remember that the construction and reinvestment markets have been buffeted and constrained by interest rate changes in the period, which have little to do with rent stabilization, the pattern suggests that these markets have discounted for stabilization and for perceptions of the likelihood of changes in city policy. The flow of investment funds has recovered accordingly, despite interest rates that continue to be very high by historical standards.

Perceptions of the quality of the neighborhoods where rental housing is located are at least holding firm and seem to be becoming more positive inside the city than in the unstabilized areas outside it. The incidence of units perceived in need of repair is rising but, again, no faster inside the city than in jurisdictions that do not regulate rents.

The Adoption of a New Adjustment Formula

Our study analyzed not only the status of landlords and tenants but also the probable effects of six alternatives to regulating the maximum rent increase permitted by the ordinance to be charged to a tenant household that had not vacated its unit. These are:

1. The continuation of the flat 7 percent ceiling then in effect
2. Variation in the rent increase according to general price inflation, as measured by the Consumer Price Index (CPI)
3. Variation in the rent increase according to the portion of the CPI that refers to prices of goods and services other than housing
4. Variation in the rent increase according to the fraction of the CPI that corresponds to the ratio of average operating costs plus profit to building income
5. Variation according to the actual average increase in building operating costs
6. A fair rate of return on investment as an allowable increase, as measured by yields on competing investments other than real estate

With respect to the 7 percent ceiling the fact is that, averaged over the entire period, the effect of that ceiling turned out to be roughly the same as would have occurred if rent increases had been permitted to rise by the change in the CPI. The average annual increase that would have occurred using the All Item CPI from 1977 to 1984 was 7.97 percent. By 1984, however, the 7 percent number was much higher than the CPI measure of the current inflation rate, then at about 4 percent.

The fair rate of return formula assumed that the pretax return on value should be equal to the weighted average of the then current mortgage interest rate and the interest rate on risky, low-grade (Baa) municipal bonds. It turned out that no standard measure of competitive investment yield had grown more rapidly in recent years than Los Angeles rental properties have appreciated in value. Neither have many stabilized properties been unprofitable. The combination of appreciation and profit regularly exceeded all competing rates of return suggested. In 1983, for example, average returns amounted to about 17 percent, considerably higher than the 12 percent average of mortgage interest and municipal bond rates. This relatively high rate was mainly due to the appreciation in property values in Los Angeles, which rose more than 11 percent.

The other four formulas broke into two types: those that vary with the general price index and those that vary with measures of trends in building costs. The two formulas within each type track closely. The difference between the two types is that those based on cost would permit rent increases just under 60 percent as great as those based on the price index. If 1985 inflation experience is similar to 1984, however, none of the four would permit rent increases as high as would continuation of the 7 percent ceiling. The cost-based formulas would permit 1985 raises of about 2.25 percent, while the price index based formulas would allow maximum increases of about 4 percent.

In June 1985 the Los Angeles city council considered these alternatives.[9] When the debate started, owners asked for adoption of a cost-based formula to reflect the real increases in their operating costs. By the time the debate ended, owners were urging that the council retain the 7 percent figure or move to a formula based on the CPI. Tenants, who had begun by favoring the CPI, now observed that the cost-based formulas permitted the smallest increases and urged its adoption.

The Rent Stabilization Division cautioned the council to consider relative ease of administration as an additional criteria along with the cost implications for landlords and tenants. Since formulas based on indices of the behavior of building costs would require a reliable and regularly updated base of data about trends in those costs, they would involve considerable expense for the city. This factor, among others, led the staff to recommend the CPI, which would require that only one number be determined each year from an easily available national index compiled at another level of government. In June 1985 the council adopted the CPI as the new rent adjustment basis, limiting it to a ceiling of no more than 8 percent per year and a floor of no less than 3 percent. That means that owners can raise rents by 4 percent in the next year. This alternative was adopted by a vote of 12–2, a perhaps surprising degree of unanimity for an issue so hard fought.[10]

The Road Ahead

The overall picture in the *rear*view mirror is one in which the Los Angeles rental housing market has traversed peaks and valleys to emerge at roughly the point that it would have reached without rent stabilization. The policy has made a major difference in the distribution of the rent burden among tenants and in the financial impact on owners in any year or succession of years. But the changing economic context has tended to even out these fluctuations over time. The quick approval of the amendment to the rent-setting formula in 1985 is probably an indication that rent control is headed toward the bottom of the council agenda for the time being in Los Angeles. Of course, if the nation endures another round of high inflation, raising the consumer price index and taking rents up too, the debate may well begin again.

Notes

1. Community Analysis and Planning Division, city of Los Angeles.

2. A brief history of this period can be found in "Rent Control in Los Angeles: A Response to Proposition 13," case study prepared by Jeffrey I. Chapman for the Intercollegiate Case Clearing House, 1981.

3. These were defined as units where on May 31, 1978, rents were at least: $302 for a unit with no bedroom; $420 for a unit with one bedroom; $588 for a unit with two bedrooms; $756 for a unit with three bedrooms; and $823 for a unit with four bedrooms.

4. This was defined as housing located in a structure for which a certificate of occupancy was first issued after October 1, 1979.

5. This was defined as spouse, children, parents, grandparents, grandchildren, brother, sister, father-in-law, mother-in-law, son-in-law, daughter-in-law, brother-in-law, or sister-in-law in the original version. Later this provision was limited to spouse, children, parents, grandparents, and grandchildren.

6. A later amendment made it possible to remove the unit from controls entirely if the unit is vacated and the landlord does renovative work costing at least $10,000 for zero bedrooms, $11,000 for one bedroom, $13,000 for two bedrooms, $15,000 for three bedrooms, and $17,000 for four or more bedrooms.

7. The consultant work was awarded to Hamilton, Rabinovitz, Szanton, and Alschuler Incorporated and to the Urban Institute. Francine Rabinovitz served as project manager for the team.

8. The cities used for comparison in the study were the largest contiguous cities that had no rent regulation. These are Torrance, Pasadena, Inglewood, Long Beach, Glendale, and Burbank.

9. The council also had before it an analysis of a number of replacements for and supplements to rent stabilization. These programs were designed to provide approximately the same net benefits delivered to target beneficiary groups by rent stabilization but through other means. They included imposition of a variety of specialized taxes. In general, all of the rates generated by the options were much higher than those that have traditionally been imposed in Los Angeles.

10. *Los Angeles Times* City-County Bureau Chief Bill Bayarsky commented: "Even the most long-winded council orators spared themselves and the audience before a surprisingly one-sided 12–2 vote in favor of a compromise continuation of the rent control law. There was a lesson in that action. The failure of the council to share the spectators' passion and the overwhelming vote showed that rent control—traditionally a controversial government intervention—is here to stay." *Los Angeles Times* (27 May 1985).

9

Last Straw or First Brick: A Commentary on Rent Control

In this chapter rental housing analysts and activists discuss the implications of rent control for tenure and vacation decontrol, for profitability of ownership, and for property rights and equity. They describe who is subsidizing whom and they summarize the politics of the rental market. And they inquire about the prospects for compromise and negotiation.

STEPHEN CARLSON: I have two concerns. What can we do in terms of an overall statewide policy to promote a perception of certainty and stability and to preclude the kind of polarization referred to earlier that takes place when the circumstances are a bit extreme?

The second question: If Los Angeles rent control has had little effect one way or the other on tenants and owners, and if it is true that if rent control were to be phased out over a lengthy period of time—five to seven years—there would be reasonably little effect, is abolition then a desirable goal?

KARL MANHEIM: We have focused on the rights of the property owners; of course, the focus of the question to a very large extent determines the analysis of the answer. Refocusing the question on the rights of tenants and the rights of persons who need housing could restructure our analysis.

Second, once the different rights and legal interests are identified, who has the responsibility for balancing these? It is easy to say that there are competing rights and competing interests and a balance must be struck. But which level of government, if any level of government, should be responsible? It is facile to say "let those rights and interests be worked out in the marketplace." That does not work because those rights only make sense in terms of some legal framework, and the legal framework is inseparable from the government's responsibility.

BARBARA ZEIDMAN: From the perspective that we have a form of rent stabilization in Los Angeles that has worked (it has met the major policy thrust of the city council at the time it was adopted) but also acknowledging that rent control systems evolve we need to discuss how we can best change the form of the regulation. How do we change regulation to better target its results? It was an amazement that it targeted as well as it did, but what do we do about the "unintended beneficiaries"—our euphemistic reference to the yuppie group that has managed to benefit from rent stabilization in Los Angeles?

Second: we must talk with landlords, and we must talk with tenants. We must talk more reasonably with each other. Housing is a very poor coalition issue; the coalition falls apart after immediate needs are met, but the need to go on in some form of solution capacity continues. It is incumbent on those who practice in this field to identify what it is that we can sit down and talk about. Where are differences so extreme that it would be fruitless to continue a dialogue? To reduce the rancorous level of debate certainly is in the city's best interest in finding reasonable policy solutions.

JOEL SILVERMAN: I object to the assumption that rent control is a fact of life. Rent control is a problem. Is not the existence of a problem an admission of failure on the part of government to provide affordable housing and to provide an economic atmosphere in which housing will be built? Is it proper, from a societal point of view or from an equity point of view, to place the cost of the rent subsidy—that is, the spread between the cost of providing housing and the proper rental level for tenants to pay—on the providers of housing? If a city or a state decides that rent control is an appropriate mechanism to provide affordable housing, should not that cost be spread equally among the population, as opposed to being borne primarily by the providers of housing? These people should be an ally of government in the effort to provide afford-able housing; instead we are alienating current and future providers of housing by increasingly restrictive rent control ordinances.

MICHAEL TEITZ: A wonderful set of questions! I would add whether it would be possible to improve the level of information that we have about the housing market in the state at large and locally. The study that we were engaged in is a marvelous example: We spent a year engaged in rancorous debate within the steering committee over certain details. Then we rushed in and collected data on a one-shot basis in essentially three months, which should have been a six- to nine-month effort. We had two months to do the analysis, which should have been a six-month effort. Fifteen months would have been a reasonable time for the study. We had to generate information that ought to be routinely available.

BARBARA ZEIDMAN: First, I'd like to respond to the observation that if rent control has no effect, why are we investing so much in pursuing this policy? I think to make that statement is to misconstrue both the impact and the statement that the study tries to make. It is true that in the aggregate rent levels in Los Angeles, compared with rent levels outside of Los Angeles, look essentially similar. But it is important to go to the next level down and to see on what groups it has had an impact and on what groups it has not had an impact. When we look at the winners and the losers, we begin to see that public policy has, to a very large extent, been met by the form of the regulation in Los Angeles. The stated policy goals were to stop rapidly escalating rents, to provide measures of security of tenure, and to provide, at the same time, a fair and reasonable return on the investment that represented the landlord's interest in the property. Did we do these things? It is basically a program that has served the elderly, small families, and the low- and the moderate-income groups in Los Angeles. It is not the fulfillment of every yuppie dream. If anything, that is who is bearing the expense.

Who is bearing the subsidy? It was not primarily an expense borne by the property owners, although they did contribute to it. It was an expense borne by other tenants, basically by the more affluent, more-mobile, and those likely to be moving upward in economic terms; that group of tenants is the one from whom the subsidy is flowing to that target group of tenants, which surprisingly (dumb luck will replace any amount of planning) is the group that has benefited in Los Angeles.

Why are we bothering? Because rent control is delivering a subsidy system, at relatively low cost, to the group whom we had in mind when the subsidy system was developed. The fact that the unintended beneficiary group is so small is a remarkable achievement for public policy.

STEPHEN CARLSON: I agree with you almost entirely. The question I raised about phasing out rent control was an analytical one, rather than a wish. We have been primary actors in a piece of legislation that would, in effect, mandate a Los Angeles form of rent control should a community opt to have rent control in California. The (Costa)* bill is a recognition that what is happening in Los Angeles generally works. Perhaps we could be a little more direct in providing assistance to those of the very lowest income who, in fact, seem to be the intended beneficiaries of the ordinance. We have amended into the bill a means of raising money to be directed at those people who really need the help. Rent control in a general sense misses the mark, particularly the most restrictive forms of rent control. Tenants need to know that their rent is not going to go up 100 percent, and landlords need to know that they can make a little profit and maintain their places. The Los Angeles kind of regulation, which is very similar to the (Costa) bill, works.

---

* A rent control bill has been introduced by Jim Costa in the California Legislature for each of the last six years.

KARL MANHEIM: To put the whole housing issue in context, we have to recognize where housing fits in the spectrum of social goods and rights. In the United States housing is not considered to be a right, certainly not a fundamental right. People do not have any claim to have decent and suitable housing. When you contrast that with fundamental rights the legal system protects, like the right of large corporations to have free speech and of people to travel interstate highways, you might begin to think that the whole notion of rights out of balance is one of the causes of the crisis of rent control.

The problem of housing has been identified by virtually every level of government. Congress found and declared that there is a shortage of adequate and affordable housing throughout the nation, especially for low- and moderate-income groups and elderly and handicapped persons. Yet, the Reagan administration, while recognizing the problem, is cutting back on means to address the problem. That fact shifts the responsibility. Should the responsibility rest with the state? California has a similar expression of policy. The early attainment of decent housing and suitable living environments for every California family is a priority of the highest order. Again, the state has recognized the housing crisis, and yet, what means does it provide for addressing that problem? We have things such as Proposition 13, which reduced funds to local government. We also have the Gann initiative, which reduced the government's ability to spend. We have other constitutional provisions that directly restrict local governments' ability to construct low-income housing. We have seen further restrictions on the ability of local government to deal with the problem.

If the problem exists and is recognized by higher levels of government, they have to start assuming some responsibility for it. And if they are not going to assume responsibility for it, then they have to leave local governments with adequate tools to deal with it. As fifty communities in the state have recognized, and many more throughout the country, rent control is a mechanism to deal with scarcity of land, the high cost of construction, and all the other governmental constraints that are imposed on the availability of housing.

LEROY GRAYMER: Could you support the position that there is, in Los Angeles, rent control that has achieved the desired objectives? Also, are the provisions in Santa Monica's ordinance necessary?

KARL MANHEIM: The problem with trying to formulate a statewide response is treating the entire state as a homogeneous entity, which it is not. Land availability differs in the state. The demographics and economics are different just between Los Angeles and Santa Monica; to try to mandate a rigid program that has the same contours irrespective

of the needs misses the point. A certain flexibility is required. That the
Los Angeles rental stabilization program works in Los Angeles does not
mean it is going to work in other parts of the state. That would be my
objection to a statewide mandate.

JOEL SILVERMAN: Property-owners, as a rule, can live with Los
Angeles-style rent control; it strikes a medium and politically it is acceptable. Ideologically, any price controls are objected to, but politically it
is acceptable. One thing people would like in Los Angeles is certainty;
not knowing which way rent control is going to go in the future is very
disconcerting to property-owners.

The Los Angeles rent control ordinance, while tolerable, has nothing
to do with that of the radical rent control cities like Berkeley, Santa
Monica, West Hollywood, and several others throughout the state. There
housing is perceived as a right. And housing may well be a right. But
housing in Santa Monica is not a right. To say "I want to live in Santa
Monica" should not be a right. I want to live in Beverly Hills, so lower
the price of houses in Beverly Hills! Is that a right?

We might differ also on what is "decent and suitable." A two-hundred-
square-foot apartment dwelling might be decent and suitable under
certain circumstances, but governments will not permit that. Also, Santa
Monica might resolve a lot of its problems of affordable housing if they
change their density allowances or quadruple the number of units zoned.
Municipalities can do that, but that does not suit their environmentalist
zeal. They want affordable housing with restrictive zoning.

MICHAEL TEITZ: I am interested in the question of property rights
because the issue is always raised as though it is a question of fact—there
are property rights or there are not property rights in classes of property.
All rights change over time. The rights of free speech in the United
States are very different now than they were during World War I or II.
We are observing a process in which some rights are slowly being redefined. My preference is not to redefine any right too fast because most
radical changes produce a set of adverse consequences.

The other question is that of subsidy. It is always said that the subsidy
is paid by the owners of the property. Let's try to work out why rents
rise and what part of the increase is attributable to what causes. In West
Los Angeles, in which there has been a rapid rise in rents over the past
five or seven years, a good part of the increase, which is a potential
windfall to owners of property, has nothing to do with their doing.
Under normal circumstances an owner would invest in property in order
to upgrade it, to attract the tenant who would be willing to pay more.
At the same time, the increase in rentability in an area like that is largely
due to market and demographic forces that are occurring for reasons

having nothing to do with the area itself. In the cases of Santa Monica and Berkeley increases in rentability might also be occurring as a result of government policy that has mandated a certain level of environmental quality: the whole environment is made more attractive, and people are willing to pay more. Those actions are producing a windfall, and what we're talking about here is who should get the benefit of the windfall and who should pay the costs that are associated with it if those benefits are fully reached? By preserving the capacity of people to at least stay where they are, rent control gives some of the benefits to those who have been in units for some length of time. In other words, we're saying to the property-owner and the tenant, "you're going to share that windfall." When the tenant leaves, the landlord can jack the rent up where there is vacancy decontrol. In a way that is a redefinition of property rights, but it's also a redefinition of what we mean by *subsidy*.

It is necessary to distinguish between the windfall potential of those situations which the Los Angeles-type ordinance deals with quite well, from situations in which entire regions have adjustment problems, with rapidly supplying housing in response to a special situation. Rent control was first implemented in wartime conditions exactly to prevent that kind of windfall gain.

KARL MANHEIM: I want to add to the windfalls identified. There are other windfalls besides zoning regulations that enhance the value of land. If we were to increase the density in Santa Monica, for instance, that would probably have a greater adverse effect on the property values of apartment owners than the economic effect of rent control. But other types of subsidies go to landlords; to characterize the problem simply as a question of why should landlords subsidize tenants is to only look at half of the economic issue. Subsidies also flow the other way.

The whole tax system is a subsidy to owners of property, to landlords in particular, through a variety of mechanisms such as depreciation allowances. Now if the federal and state governments, which are the taxing authorities, were to eliminate those types of deductions and instead achieve the same economic result by direct cash grants to landlords, then we could see that as a subsidy from the entire population to landlords and would ask, why they are being subsidized. Tenants do not receive any tax benefits from their housing payments, whereas homeowners do.

Other subsidies include what I would characterize as below-market mortgage loans to owners of property. To some extent, banks obtain their funds from below-market savings accounts of small investors, low- and moderate-income people, and in turn are able to loan out mortgage money at lower rates. So we have subsidies flowing in all directions, and to focus on any one of them, is a real mistake.

STEPHEN CARLSON: I disagree that the renter gets no subsidy. The state has a renters' credit: renters who make over $35,000 a year in rent control jurisdictions get double subsidies. I think we should get rid of that to raise a little money to direct at those who are most needy.

We are agreeing to some form of subsidy as a practical and political matter. But the level of subsidy that seems to be desired in places like Santa Monica and Berkeley goes so far beyond what seems to be fair and reasonable.

The local control argument from Santa Monica and Berkeley is a bit ludicrous because the activists who are promoting that issue were, in the past, the first ones to run to Sacramento or to Washington saying "please help us here; please help us there." Local control is a red-herring argument. Housing is of statewide importance; the state has said so, and, in fact, housing is a homogeneous product: What happens in Santa Monica affects West Hollywood, Berkeley, Oakland, and Contra Costa County. You cannot just impose an artificial political boundary, as Berkeley and Santa Monica and now West Hollywood have attempted to do.

JOEL SILVERMAN: There is a change in property rights. The distinction is between vacancy control and nonvacancy control. In areas where there are no vacancy controls, the windfalls that originated in wartime could also be called by the intelligent investor investing in growth communities; investors seek to maximize their returns.

Tax subsidies to landlords are subsidies to tenants. If you were to remove tax subsidies to landlords, investors in real property would say, "I want to get a comparable return on my investment in real estate as I would get in risk-free investments." Real estate is anything but risk free; real estate is a very management-intensive, high-risk investment. Today, throughout most of the areas of Los Angeles, even those without rent control, properties are generally sold at an illusory break-even point. Property is not sold with a return on your cash that is comparable to what you could achieve in even a Treasury bill or a savings account. You take away the tax benefits to landlords, and you are going to find a tremendous need for investors, especially those who are handling fiduciary dollars (such as syndicators and other institutional investors), to find an equal return to what is available in nonrisky, non-management-intensive areas. Initially there would be a downward pressure on prices to pick up that additional return required, but the other side of the coin is a tremendous upward pressure on rents.

BARBARA ZEIDMAN: I think there is also an additional shift of rights; the provisions for just-cause eviction: "I can live here absent the following things."

STEPHEN CARLSON: The only rational basis for just-cause eviction ordinances is the argument that vacancy decontrol creates an incentive on the part of a property-owner to remove a tenant and therefore jack up the rent. About 95 or closer to 100 percent of all evictions are for flat nonpayment of rent. There are abuses, and the trade-off, in terms of getting vacancy decontrol, is for a community to enact what it feels to be a strong and reasonable just-cause eviction ordinance. The Supreme Court of California, in the Birkenfeld case, has in essence stated that you cannot have just-cause eviction that is not tied in with an existing rent control ordinance.

LEROY GRAYMER: There seems to be a lack of clarity regarding what is being redistributed to whom under what kinds of rent control provisions. What I would like now is to learn a little more about stability factors. Do we have stability among the renters in Santa Monica? It does not seem to have the same kind of rapid turnover that exists in a vacancy decontrol situation.

KARL MANHEIM: Unfortunately I am not equipped with any hard statistics. One interesting statistic accompanied the advent of Los Angeles rent control: the incidence of just-cause evictions rose 300 percent at the time when the Los Angeles rent stabilization ordinance with vacancy decontrol was enacted. There is an incentive for landlords to take advantage of vacancy decontrol provisions. That does not, by itself, suggest that they are a bad feature. But if they provide a certain benefit to landlords ought that benefit be tied to other benefits in the overall housing picture?

There are two specific programs that I have in mind: West Hollywood has proposed a limited vacancy decontrol tied with assurances of maintenance of the apartments. Santa Monica authorized limited vacancy decontrol tied with insurance of provision of low-income housing. A landlord would be eligible for vacancy decontrol upon establishing that 15 percent of the units are occupied by low-income people. That is a way, perhaps, of targeting the beneficiaries of rent control and at the same time achieving the cash incentives that the landlords are seeking.

The absence or presence of vacancy decontrol certainly has much more of a political impact than a legal impact. Vacancy decontrol cannot be used as a mechanism to ensure the legality of any rent control law. The law has to be legal without reference to vacancy decontrol because you cannot determine whether any particular landlord is going to be able to take advantage of it. And the volatile political constituencies that exist view the issue quite differently.

JOEL SILVERMAN: West Hollywood, Santa Monica, and Berkeley have political constituencies that are overwhelmingly renters. We have to acknowledge that what we are dealing with is not an ideological economic redistribution to provide affordable housing. What we are dealing with is the development of a political constituency. Every time an apartment turns over and that unit is no longer granting a new tenant a below-market subsidy, then politicians who run on the issue of rent control have lost a vote. That is why condominium conversions have been cut off and a whole series of other factors of the law have been enacted. If we want to deal with just-cause eviction as an issue, why not allow the rent control board in place to supervise just-cause evictions? If just-cause evictions are an issue, face it head on!

The other thing you have to consider when dealing with radical rent control is what it does to the perceived value of the property in real economic terms. *Gross rental multipliers* is the term that describes how real estate is traded. Prior to the enactment of rent control, to buy in West Hollywood you had to pay 8½ or maybe 8¾ times the rent that the building was generating. After the enactment of rent control, the upside potential was greatly limited and the gross multiplier dropped dramatically; the future earnings of the building are discounted. Now you have a situation where the value of the building has dropped from an 8½ multiplier down to a 6½ or 7 multiplier. For a recent purchaser that 20 percent drop can represent the entire equity in the building. For a $1 million building a 20 percent decrease will wipe out the two-hundred-thousand-dollar down payment that that purchaser has put into that building—that's a complete wipeout of equity. The other unfair thing is it wipes out the retirement equity of elderly owners who perceived the equity in their building as being there even if they never raised the rent on their tenants. They always knew that subsequent buyers would pay a premium for the building because they had the ability to raise rents to market at some future date. Taking away that ability, you have dramatically reduced the equity of these elderly owners.

AUDIENCE QUESTION: What would happen if we drop rent control?

MICHAEL TEITZ: A lot depends on methods. You have to think not about yes or no, but about how. If, for example, it were phased out over a five-year period or a seven-year period, then the effects, probably, would be relatively modest over the long haul. However, some of the people who are benefiting now in certain markets would find themselves forced out over that period; there would be some real costs. If it were phased out overnight, I think the political firestorm would consume city hall, and it would be back the following day.

FRANCINE RABINOVITZ: Politics can often dominate economic reasoning. If that is the case, then one ought not to talk about abolition or retention but focus seriously on what are the legitimate alternatives for the groups that are now being helped. There is a group in the population that is being helped, and if the goal is abolition, then the discussion ought to center around legitimate alternative programs that might be put forward to serve the needs of that group.

AUDIENCE COMMENT: Mr. Teitz talked of property rights being redefined. I think he is a semanticist. I think it would be more accurate to say they are being eroded.

MICHAEL TEITZ: Property rights truly are redefined where you increase one group's property rights at the expense of decreasing another's. We are producing a new kind of property right in tenure; that is, a right that is associated with the amount of time you have been somewhere rather than a right associated with what historically has been termed *legal ownership*. And there are many such rights that exist. So I used the term *redefinition* quite consciously. There is erosion on one side, but at the same time there is a certain gain on the other and that is indeed a political process. I am not suggesting that it is good or bad, but it is there.

AUDIENCE QUESTION: Do any of you have any ideas about how you could build a broader political constituency for rental housing on the federal, state, or local level in a more constructive way?

BARBARA ZEIDMAN: A broad-based political constituency is eight votes on the city council.

Housing is not an issue that lends itself to a good political constituency because the pulling within that group is so diverse. The constituency that exists in rent-stabilized or rent-controlled communities is not for housing production. On a theoretical level it might be, but what I hear in the practicalities of doing rent stabilization is the politics of greed, not the politics of need. That comes from both the landlord's side of the house and the tenant's side of the house.

MICHAEL TEITZ: Rent control is a blunt instrument, and one cannot expect too much of it.

KARL MANHEIM: I would elevate the right to housing, at least to be on a par with the right to education. The constituency for decent education for everyone in this country is a very broad-based one, and if we viewed housing with equal dignity, we might see the constituency for decent housing also.

LEROY GRAYMER: Are there any other points that panel members would like to make?

STEPHEN CARLSON: The issue is really one of supply: it is the issue of creating a housing policy that all the speakers said does not exist in the nation, although it exists a little bit in California. The problem needs to be addressed on a comprehensive basis. The forum should be brought to the state level, where the dialogue is still volatile but not quite so volatile as it is on the local level.

MICHAEL TEITZ: We have learned a few things about rent control in the last ten or fifteen years. It is possible to design a form of regulation that is not disastrous. We lack principally in the capacity for rational discussion to arrive at that, which means essentially the willingness to negotiate and compromise.

BARBARA ZEIDMAN: No matter how well thought out in the council chambers or in academic symposiums, public policy that does not make sense to the public is no policy whatsoever. The fact is that at least in Los Angeles we can make rent control work because we can make people understand it. They do not have to agree with it, but they must understand why you did it.

JOEL SILVERMAN: Speaking as the owner of property in an area where landlords are hopelessly outnumbered as voters, there simply is not any equity to be had on the local level. This is a trend—more and more cities are finding themselves subjected to radical rent control. Regardless of your point of view, there is no compromise possible when there is no objective forum in which compromise can be heard. There is only hope on the state level; there is no hope on the local level, as is illustrated by the frustration of many of the people who are landlords in radical rent control areas.

KARL MANHEIM: I will use my closing remarks to simply read a passage from a very recent case by the California Court of Appeal:

> In the last ten years, urban areas in California have begun to find essentially all vacant land filled, with little or no vacant space for the installation of additional housing. In many of California's largest cities, virtually no empty space exists which is available for additional housing. Given California's continued population growth, it is just a matter of time before the remaining vacant space will be exhausted in every major city in California. Unless or until the legislature determines this issue to be a proper subject of general state law, local government will be under increasing pressure to adopt rent control as a means of protecting its citizens from excessive rent resulting from increased shortages of rental housing.

Index

San Francisco County, 49
San Francisco Plan, 7
San Joaquin Valley, 49
San Jose County, 49
Santa Barbara County, 49; new
    construction in, 46
Santa Monica, 108, 109, 110, 111;
    percentage of renters in, 4, 14;
    political constituencies in, 112–
    113; rent control in, 88, 93;
    vacancy decontrol in, 112
Scarcity rents, 89
Seven counties; new construction in,
    46, 47; trends in, 48
Shortage, 31–32
Simpson-Mazzoli bill, 38
Single-family houses; inventory of,
    29–30; ownership of, 1979, 13
South coast region, rental vacancy
    rate in, 31
Southern California, new
    construction in, 44–45
Speculative boom, 35
State housing finance agencies, 23
Structure types, 29–30
Subsidies, 20–22, 26, 49, 54, 110;
    federal, 17–18; rent control as,
    107; renter's credit as, 111; tax
    system as, 110
Supply, 4–5; boomlets and, 41–42;
    prospective, 36–39. *See also*
    Construction, new; Market
    trends, current
Supply objectives, 12–14
Surplus land, 69
Surplus units, 23

Tax benefits, 15–17, 22, 26, 59; to
    homeowners, 21; to landlords,
    111; and new construction, 58,

62; proposed, 23; as subsidy to
    property owners, 110
Tenants; costs to, 34, 35; as political
    constituencies, 112–113; Los
    Angeles rent stabilization
    program and, 99–100; renter's
    credit, 111
Tenure of tenancy, 88; and subsidy,
    100
Thrift institutions, 15, 16, 17
Townhouses, 35
Transportation, impact of housing
    policy on, 63

UCLA-Graduate School of
    Management forecasts, 41

Vacancy control, 111, 112
Vacancy rate, 31, 63–64, 97;
    interpretation of data, 60; Los
    Angeles rent stabilization
    program and, 100; rent control
    and, 89
Ventura County, 45, 49; multifamily
    housing percentage, 49
Very-low-income groups;
    consumption trends, 55;
    definitions, 25
Voucher program, 22, 23

West Hollywood, and just cause
    evictions, 108; nature of rent
    control program, 112–113
Windfall gain, 110

Yuppies, 56, 106

Zoning, 7, 18–19, 76; as factor in case
    study, 67; in Los Angeles
    County, 62